Warrior Women

Warrior Women

The Amazons of Dahomey and the Nature of War

ROBERT B. EDGERTON

University of California Los Angeles

Westview Press
A Member of the Perseus Books Group

Copyright © 2000 by Westview Press, A Member of the Perseus Books Group

Published in 2000 in the United States of America by Westview Press, 5500 Central Avenue, Boulder, Colorado 80301–2877, and in the United Kingdom by Westview Press, 12 Hid's Copse Road, Cumnor Hill, Oxford OX2 9JJ

Find us on the World Wide Web at www.westviewpress.com

Library of Congress Cataloging-in-Publication Data
Edgerton, Robert B., 1931–
    Warrior women : the Amazons of Dahomey and the nature of war / Robert B. Edgerton.
        p. cm.
    Includes bibliographical references and index.
    ISBN 0-8133-3711-9 (hc)
    1. Women soldiers—Benin—History—19th century.   2. Women, Fon.
3. Benin—History, Military—19th century.   I. Title.

UB419.B46 E34   2000
355'.0082'096683—dc21

                                                                00-026134

The paper used in this publication meets the requirements of the American National Standard for Permanence of Paper for Printed Library Materials Z39.48–1984.

10   9   8   7   6   5   4   3   2   1

Contents

Acknowledgments

As with any book that has been a long time in the making, this one owes much to people who are too numerous to mention. In addition to scores of graduate students in my anthropology classes at UCLA over the past few years, I would especially like to thank Orna Johnson, Jorja Prover, Keith Otterbein, Tom Weisner, Wally Goldschmidt, Alan Fiske, and Doug Hollan for their helpful suggestions. Special thanks are due to Rob Williams, my editor at Westview Press, for his many thoughtful comments on earlier drafts of the book, and to Margaret Ritchie for her superb copy-editing.

I am grateful for the kindness and courtesy of the librarians at the British Museum, the British Public Records Office (Kew), the Bodleian Library of Oxford University, the Centre des Archives d'Outre-Mer in Aix-en-Provence, and especially the Inter-library Loan Department of the Charles E. Young Research Library at the University of California, Los Angeles. This book could never have been completed without the research assistance and manuscript preparation of Paula L. Wilkinson, R. Jean Cadigan, and Patricia A. Tilburg. Bravo! Along with Marta L. Wilkinson, Patricia Tilburg also helped greatly with translations of some French materials, something Linda Soares did for some Portuguese publications. Thanks, too, to Sharon Belkin for drawing the map.

Finally, although I have made use of primary materials such as journals, letters, and books of Europeans who visited Dahomey as well as some British and French government documents, I have also relied heavily on the work of past and present scholars, whose work did much to ease my journey into the complexities of

Dahomey. Their published work is cited in the bibliography and I offer here my thanks. I would particularly like to call readers' attention to two recent books. *Amazons of Black Sparta* by Stanley Alpern was published in 1998 after I had completed an earlier, and longer, draft of this book. Mr. Alpern's detailed treatment of the Amazons made it possible for me to reduce much of the detail in my book that was not directly relevant to the issues I wanted to emphasize. Interested readers are encouraged to refer to Alpern's book for a broader discussion of the Amazons than I provide. I also want to acknowledge my intellectual debt to historian Edna G. Bay, whose writings have done more than those of anyone else to help me understand the world of Dahomean women. Readers will find much of interest in her latest book, *Wives of the Leopard*, published in 1998.

My greatest debt is to my wife, Karen Ito, not only for her perceptive anthropological criticism of the manuscript but for making everything worthwhile.

Robert B. Edgerton

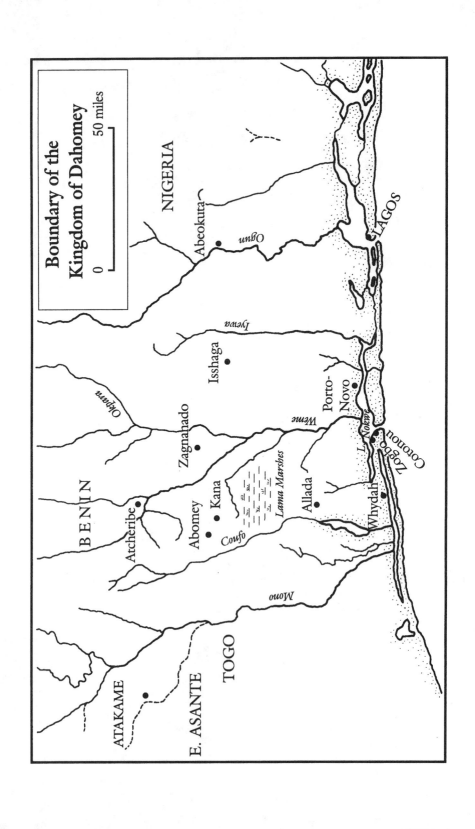

Boundary of the
Kingdom of Dahomey

0   50 miles

NIGERIA

Abeokuta

Ogun

LAGOS

Iyewa

Isshaga

Okpara

Porto-
Novo

Weme

Zagnanado

BENIN

Nokwe

Cotonou

Zogbo

Atcheribe

Kana

Lama Marshes

Abomey

Allada

Whydah

Coufo

Mono

ATAKAME

TOGO

E. ASANTE

Introduction

John Keegan is one of the most respected military historians of our time with numerous books to his credit, including perhaps his most important one, *A History of Warfare*, published in 1993. This otherwise commendable exploration into many dimensions of war ends its opening chapter with the startling conclusion that although women are said sometimes to be able to become "messianic war leaders,"

> warfare is, nevertheless, the one human activity from which women, with the most insignificant exceptions, have always and everywhere stood apart. Women look to men to protect them from danger, and bitterly reproach them when they fail as defenders. Women have followed the drum, nursed the wounded, tended the fields and herded the flocks when the man of the family has followed his leader, have even dug the trenches for men to defend and laboured in the workshops to send them their weapons. Women, however, do not fight. They rarely fight among themselves and they never, in any military sense, fight men. If warfare is as old as history and as universal as mankind, we must now enter the supremely important limitation that it is an entirely masculine activity.[1]

In that same year, another well-regarded historian, Martin Van Creveld of Hebrew University and a former Fellow of War Studies at King's College, Cambridge, agreed with Keegan: "Women have never taken part in combat—in any culture, in any country, in any period of history. The myth of Amazons is just that—a myth."[2]

That Keegan and Van Creveld could reach this conclusion is remarkable in view of the fact that British popular historian John Laffin wrote a book called *Women in Battle* as early as 1967, which, if sometimes embellished, nonetheless provided considerable evidence that women have fought against men in many times and many places. And Laffin was hardly alone. Although most military historians have neglected women's exploits as warriors, there has long been ample evidence to demonstrate that in many parts of the world, some women have taken up arms and engaged in combat, sometimes alone, sometimes in the company of men, and sometimes side-by-side with other women. To contradict Keegan's declaration, historian Linda Grant De Pauw wrote *Women in War from Prehistory to the Present: Battle Cries and Lullabies* in 1998.[3] A year earlier, anthropologist David E. Jones wrote *Women Warriors: A History*, a book that, like De Pauw's, systematically summarized the many ways in which some women have "always and everywhere" *not* stood apart from warfare.[4] Broad surveys like those by Jones and De Pauw cannot be expected to place women's wartime activities in cultural context, nor to explain why women have not fought in many parts of the world, but they do demonstrate that in many cultures for much of recorded history, women have fought in combat.

Women have not engaged in warfare at all times and in all places, but they have fought bravely and well in many times and in many places, and in one society, the Kingdom of Dahomey in Benin, West Africa, full-time professional women soldiers fought so ferociously and successfully for so many years that they eventually became the elite force of Dahomey's professional, highly successful standing army. They became the scourge of Dahomey's many enemies, and those who saw them in action, including French Foreign Legionnaires and Marine Infantry who fought against them during the 1890s, said that they were not only far superior to Dahomey's excellent professional male soldiers, but every bit the equal of those proud French soldiers.[5]

In his 1999 book, the *Dark Side of Man*, after a well-reasoned review of the origins of male violence, including much documentation that violence comes naturally to males, biological anthropologist Michael P. Ghiglieri has convincingly argued that male bonding is a natural and necessary feature of men's success in combat. But he then concluded that "history reveals no armies of women bonded into the 'do-or-die' military units vital to win in combat."[6] Although it is true that such intense female bonding is rare, it has, in fact, occurred. During most of the nineteenth century and perhaps even earlier, the full-time women soldiers of Dahomey were bonded in as "do-or-die" a military unit as the world has ever seen.

In examining the lives of Dahomean women in the eighteenth and nineteenth centuries we must rely primarily on the books, journals, and letters of European explorers, military men, missionaries, government officials, and traders, including slave traders from Britain, France, Holland, and Portugal. More recently, historians, anthropologists, and other scholars, including a few from Benin itself, have contributed to our understanding of the kingdom and its women, but no Dahomean woman was interviewed until 1920, so we were left with an almost exclusively male-centered perspective.[7] During the last half of the twentieth century, a number of fine historians wrote valuable, insightful works on various aspects of the preconquest kingdom. Edna G. Bay's recent book, *Wives of the Leopard*, for example, should be required reading for anyone with an interest in Dahomey.[8] But the firsthand observations of Europeans before Dahomey's ultimate defeat—and social reshaping—by the French, were written by men whose motives and powers of observation varied.

Some of those who wrote about Dahomey in the eighteenth and nineteenth centuries expressed favorable views about the kingdom, but many were enthusiasts of the slave trade who attempted to justify it by portraying Dahomean culture as unspeakably brutal and barbaric, arguing that slaves sent to the New World were far better off than most people who remained in Dahomey. Others were priests or ministers, who were almost obligated to find fault with Dahomean religion. Still others had political agendas involving eventual European control over the kingdom. Most of these men felt superior to any African, and some who wrote about Dahomey were ardently committed to the racist doctrine that Africans were inferior to Europeans in every way.

Exceptions were few, but there were some. British surgeon John M'Leod wrote in 1820 that Dahomeans clearly "possess, in the common affairs of life, a degree of shrewdness, reasonableness, and sound sense, far beyond the natives inhabiting the barbarous portions either of Asia or America."[9] Another British visitor in the 1840s described Dahomey's King Gezo as follows: "I left him with the conviction on my mind, that he is a man of superior intellect, and endowed with an extraordinary capacity for government. . . . His mind is active and inquiring, and he betrays a laudable anxiety to be made acquainted with the laws, manners, and customs of foreign nations."[10] But favorable comments like these were not common. Many visitors agreed with the famous explorer Sir Richard Burton that the people of Dahomey, like all Africans, had limited intelligence and had made no contributions to civilization.

Captain Sir Richard Francis Burton, early in his life an officer of the army of the Honorable East India Company, was undeniably brilliant. Although mostly self-taught—he was sent down from Oxford after only a year for disobedience—he spoke some twenty-nine languages, some of them so fluently that he could pass as a native. Tall and darkly handsome (as a child some thought him a Gypsy), Burton was seldom at ease with the world, particularly Africa, where he had experienced much grief, including almost losing his life to spear-throwing natives on one occasion. Often addicted to alcohol, opium, and marijuana, not to mention frequent sexual adventures with native women around the world, including various parts of Africa, the often impatient and always vain Burton was greatly annoyed by the reception he received from the Dahomean king Glele when Britain sent him to Dahomey in 1863 with a mission to end the slave trade, not a subject the king cared to discuss.[11]

Soon after, Burton wrote two long volumes about his visit and the many faults of the Dahomeans, who, like all Africans, he described as unintelligent due to their "smaller, less convoluted" brains. He also noted that as they grew older their already limited brain power actually lessened.[12] On another occasion, speaking to the Anthropological Society of London, Burton declared that with the admixture of "northern blood," "pure Negroes" would be "improved off the face of the earth."[13] Not all visitors to Dahomey were as passionately racist as Burton—Dutch and French visitors of that era who wrote about their experiences in Dahomey were usually less rabid—but most Europeans of that time had no doubts about their own superior intelligence, and few believed that Africans, including the Fon people of Dahomey, had achieved anything of value throughout their history. Perhaps the ultimate expression of this view was put forward by Thomas Carlyle in 1849, when he declared that Africans were not inferior by chance but had been divinely created as inferior in order to serve their white masters.[14]

Most European visitors to Dahomey harbored some sense of racial superiority, and few had any sense of African history. Many of these men, perhaps even all of them, would no doubt have been surprised to learn that agriculture was first invented 70,000 years ago in southern Africa, or that the largest single piece of stone ever hewn on earth marked a grave in the ancient Ethiopian city of Aksum.[15] It weighed over 700 tons and was one of hundreds of obelisks created there. Aksum lay high in the mountains of Ethiopia at the same latitude north of the equator as the ancient city of Timbuktu in the Western Sudan. Aksum had a written language originally derived from an Arab language spoken across the Red Sea, but later so modified that it became Ge'ez, the predecessor of the modern Ethiopian script. Although Europeans usually believed that no African society had a written language, written languages also evolved in West Africa. The Vai of Liberia invented their own system of writing modeled after European examples, and the southeastern Igbo and their neighbors created an original written language that owed nothing to European or Arab languages. Called *Nsibidi*, the language was made up not of letters, but of symbols standing for concepts, much as in Chinese.[16] In some societies, powerful men blocked the education of African children by Europeans for fear that should they become literate, the traditional practices of stealing wealth from the royal treasury could no longer be maintained.[17]

It is now generally acknowledged that before European conquest, many African societies created and maintained social institutions that were as efficient as any seen on earth, just as they developed values and religious beliefs that were as complex, abstract, and meaningful as those found anywhere. It was in the realm of material culture that their achievements fell behind those of Europeans, Asians, or even Native Americans. They only rarely built monumental cities like those of the Aztec or the Inca, nor did they build oceangoing ships, and their tools and weapons were relatively simple. Many Europeans joined Richard Burton in ascribing this underdevelopment of material culture to a lack of intelligence, a conclusion that is not borne out by the evidence.

Why African societies did not develop more complex technology is a subject for continuing debate, but it is clear that this failure was not due to a lack of ability. To take but one example, all along the coast of West Africa, local blacksmiths quickly learned to repair the intentionally defective muskets that Europeans traded for slaves or gold. These blacksmiths became so adept in mastering this foreign technology, including tempering locks and brazing barrels, that French traders concluded that they did so "incomparably better than any they had ever seen."[18] In fact, many blacksmiths, including those at the coastal ports of Dahomey, were so skilled that the need to trade with Europeans for guns fell dramatically. Some blacksmiths in Dahomey even manufactured muskets and made their own gunpowder, a development that the French greeted with stark incredulity. In 1892, however, the French found convincing evidence of Dahomean inventiveness when they captured a "veritable pyrotechnic workshop" filled with gunpowder in hermetically sealed jars, cartridge cases, signal rockets, electric batteries, and the tools used to repair and make guns.[19]

Those few European visitors who wrote in praise of Africans' intelligence often referred to their impressive facility with European languages. A Portuguese visitor, F. T. Valdez, concluded, "They are in general intelligent, and somehow learn to speak, read and write different languages, especially Portuguese with which they are most conversant; some of them can speak fluently in Portuguese, Dutch, Danish, English, and even French."[20] Four decades before Valdez's visit, a British visitor was similarly amazed by the ability of a Dahomean coastal official to speak fluent English, French, and Portuguese.[21] The ability of Africans to master not only European languages but multiple African languages as well impresses foreign visitors to this day.

The first mention of coastal West Africa in the literate world was by Arabs in 1773–1774 who referred to the Kingdom of Ghana as the "land of gold."[22] But even earlier than that, West Africa was known to some visitors as a place of civilization. As early as 1,600 years ago, at Jenne-jeno, southwest of Timbuktu, a city housing at least 27,000 people was established. Surrounded by a large wall, it peaked in population in 800 A.D. and was followed by several other kingdoms that favorably impressed sophisticated Arab visitors. All had cities, kingship, well-organized governments, and complex systems of trade and taxation. Later, some of these West African kingdoms amazed Arab visitors, including the famous explorer Ibn Battuta, who had previously traveled to both China and India. When he visited Mali in 1337, Ibn Battuta was enormously impressed by its army of 100,000 men with 10,000 cavalry, and by the efficiency of their government.

> The Negroes are seldom unjust, and have a greater abhorrence of injustice than any other people. Their ruler shows no mercy to anyone who is guilty of the least act of it. There is complete security in their country. Neither traveller nor inhabitant in it has anything to fear from robbers or men of violence.[23]

At the time of Ibn Battuta's visit, Mali was one of the largest empires in the world, one so wealthy that its king readily assembled

8,000 retainers for a trip to Cairo on his way to Mecca. He arrived with so much gold that his visit devalued Egyptian goods by some 12 percent.[24] Mali eventually lost its ascendancy to neighboring states such as Songhay and Borno in the Western Sudan, and slowly, much later, states began to take shape in the forested regions along the coast of West Africa. These fledgling societies slowly grew in numbers and strength at about the time that the Portuguese rounded Cape Verde in 1445, finally building Cape Castle at Elmina on the so-called Gold Coast of what is now Ghana in 1482. The slave trade was soon to follow, bringing the people of West Africa, including the Fon people of Dahomey, onto the world stage. What set Dahomey apart from other African societies was not only its success in controlling the slave trade but also the power it gave to women, particularly in public life and, most of all, in its full-time professional army. These women would come to be known to Europeans as "Amazons."

Greek tales of Amazons—fierce nomadic women with their right breasts removed to enhance their ability as archers—like tales of similarly ferocious women reported to have lived in South America's tropical forest, have long titillated imaginations around the world despite the lack of any persuasive evidence of their actual existence. Christopher Columbus and Sir Walter Raleigh, among others, reported stories about armed women in the Caribbean and Guyana but apparently never actually saw any. However, there is credible archeological evidence to suggest that women were successful warriors across much of Libya and the steppes of southern Russia.[25] And there is no doubt that Celtic women often fought ferociously as Roman soldiers reported: "You should see these viragos, neck veins swollen with rage, swinging their robust and snow-white arms, using their feet and their fists and landing blows that seem triggered off by a catapult."[26] All of these women have sometimes been referred to as Amazons.

Whether based on the martial prowess of Celtic or other warlike women, as Abby Wettan Kleinbaum has narrated in her book, *The War Against the Amazons*, the European imagination has feasted on ideas of ferocious women warriors—"Amazons"—since Greek and Roman times. Historical claims of their existence in various parts of the world led to plays, poems, and books exalting them not only as warriors but as women of great erotic attraction for men. Some Europeans rejected the idea that a society of Amazons living without men could have existed, but German Romantics like von Kleist, Goethe, and Schiller led Europe in its obsession with Amazons as not only the utmost romantic challenge but the essence of untamed nature. Heinrich von Kleist's 1808 play, *Penthesilea,* centered on a "ferocious and bestial" woman warrior who was at the same time a "gorgeous desirable woman."[27]

Freud later speculated freely about such approach-avoidance, love-hate relationships in the nature of the human psyche, but Swiss social theorist J. J. Bachofen gave European readers an even greater jolt when he wrote *Das Mutterrect* (1861), in which he asserted that all humans once lived in societies dominated by Amazons. His image of early societies as "matriarchies" led by warrior women was controversial even at the time, and modern evolutionary theory has long rejected Bachofen's speculations. But during the latter part of the nineteenth century, when numerous Europeans were in close contact with the women soldiers of Dahomey, his ideas about women's warlike nature were on the minds of most educated people, including some who visited Dahomey.[28] Well before French troops killed Dahomey's women soldiers almost to the last woman, European visitors dubbed them Amazons, and the name has remained. Whether or not they should be called Amazons today is debatable, but there is abundant evidence of the existence of Dahomean women soldiers with exceptional martial ardor and military skills.

The questions this book will address are complex and, as in most matters of history, not answerable to everyone's satisfaction. Why did Dahomey not only give women economic and political power but, perhaps alone among the world's societies, also empower them as the elite force of a powerful professional army? The answers to these questions are not only of historical interest; they also address contemporary issues of gender hierarchy, especially those regarding the feasibility and propriety of using women in combat in modern military forces.

To pursue these questions, we begin with an introduction to the Amazons themselves: Who were they, how were they trained, what was their role in warfare? We then examine Dahomean society and culture, especially its political system, the role of women, and the monarchy. We next examine the means used to create the impression of kingly majesty and autocracy, cornerstones of Dahomean society and its military success. Next we describe the Amazons' heroic successes as well as losing campaigns during the second half of the nineteenth century. Finally, we turn to explanations for the Amazons' emergence in Dahomey and ask whether their accomplishments have implications for women—and men—today.

1

The Amazons of Dahomey

To understand the emergence of women as the elite of their warlike society, a brief look back at the history of Dahomey is indispensable. Trailing after Portuguese ships that arrived during the latter half of the fifteenth century, traders from several European nations sailed up and down the West African coast. Amused by the antics of children and adults alike who sported in the shallow surf like dolphins, they were also impressed by the skill of so-called *kruman*, African sailors recruited from hundreds of miles away to paddle their canoes out to the great ships and back to shore filled with precious cargo and terrified passengers despite towering waves and ravenous sharks so dangerous that local people would not risk venturing beyond the shallow water near the shoreline. The surf and sharks were especially dangerous at the port of Whydah on Dahomey's coast, where a Dutch slave trader named William Bosman wrote in 1698 that canoes overturned there every day. During the few weeks that Bosman spent at Whydah, seven Europeans drowned or were eaten by sharks. The victims included two English and one Portuguese sea captains.[1] But as dangerous as this coast could be, Europeans continued their explorations along it as well as their pursuit of slaves. The demands of Brazilian sugar plantations for more slaves accelerated during the 1630s, and eventually one-fifth of all slaves taken to the New World would come from coastal ports on Dahomey's aptly named "Slave Coast."[2]

Along most of the West African coast, the palm trees that studded the shoreline quickly gave way to dense tropical rain forest. The only place along this coast where open grasslands replaced the rain forest was the so-called Gap of Benin, and it was there that the Kingdom of Dahomey began to take shape about the same time that the *Mayflower* landed in what would become Massachusetts. Three miles inland, beyond palms, palmyras, a twenty-foot-high sand bank, and a shallow lagoon filled with succulent fish that tasted like trout, lay the town of Whydah (later spelled variously as "Ouidah" by the French and "Fida" by the Dutch). Although so plagued by mosquitoes that European visitors often had to take opium in order to sleep, Whydah was a pleasant, orderly town surrounded by luxuriant vegetation and remarkably fertile fields during its heyday as a slave-trading center during the eighteenth century. However, the town fell into decay as the slave trade dried up by the middle of the nineteenth century, when Whydah became a filthy, ramshackle sprawl of unkempt houses and abandoned forts. Even so, it was ruled as always with an iron hand by the Dahomean viceroy, known as the *Yovogan,* who was judge and jury and did not suffer Europeans gladly. The city once held 50,000 people, but by the mid-1800s it was reduced to 12,000 or 15,000 souls, many of them adroit thieves who stole everything of value they could lay their hands on. A British army officer who visited at this time wrote, "The natives of Whydah are the most depraved and unprincipled villains in all Africa, or perhaps the world."[3] Fortunately for the Europeans, the Yovogan permitted no violence.

The climate of Dahomey was relatively cool, thanks to the winds that blew from the north, and it was also comparatively dry, with an annual rainfall of only about 30 inches even at the coast, whereas the rest of the West African coastline usually received as much as 120 inches. When rain did fall in Dahomey, however, it could do so in torrents accompanied by thunder and lightning. Despite occasional storms, Dahomey was so relatively dry and cool that cereal crops such as millet and maize thrived, and during the fierce Harmattan winds that often roared out of the northern desert from December through February for several days at a time, even the usually humid coast became so dry that everything was desiccated. People could scarcely swallow, and little could be seen through the fine dust particles that clouded the air.

European visitors to Dahomey's capital city of Abomey, some sixty miles inland, often described the weather there as delightful. They praised the cool, clean air and approvingly noted the absence of mosquitoes. Once the viceroy at Whydah approved their travel plans, European visitors assembled a throng of more-or-less manageable male and female porters and hammock carriers, a host of supplies and gifts for the king that at various times included fine silver, coats of mail, a rocking chair, a chamber organ, a four-poster bed with silk damask curtains, and a sedan chair of red Moroccan leather, along with many worthless trinkets. But there were also some remarkable gifts. Not only did some visitors give fine carriages to the king, sometimes along with horses, but Brazilian slavers delivered a fully-rigged, twenty-foot-long model of a brigantine with every detail in place, including miniature cannon. The king was also given a forty-foot-tall circular, red damask silk tent.[4] As the time came to leave the coast for the journey inland, the Europeans lay down in hammocks and were hoisted into the air, and a party of 50 to 100 men, along with numbers of women and children, many carrying loads on their heads, set off toward the king's capital of Abomey, the hammock men capable of jogging five miles an hour, the women and children chattering happily despite their loads.

Abomey lay inland across stagnant pools, marshes, swamps, clumps of dense forest, and extensive areas of grassland that grew well over human height. The soil was immensely fertile red loam with no rocks to be found, not even pebbles, until Abomey was reached. The major rivers in the kingdom paralleled the usually smooth caravan route to the north rather than crossing it, making travel relatively easy. The elevation increased slightly as the visitors moved north, but there were no mountains to climb and even hills were rarely found anywhere in the kingdom. As the caravan moved north, many beautiful, fragrant flowers were seen, especially lilies, along with thousands of large butterflies and hordes of large reddish bats that sometimes swarmed like gnats.[5] Most wildlife tended to stay out of the path of large traveling parties, but snakes were seen, including so-called "boa constrictors"—actually pythons—said to be anywhere from twenty to thirty feet long.[6] Birds of all sorts abounded, including edible ones such as quail, partridges, doves, pigeons, guinea hens, and turkeys. During the day, visitors heard monkeys chattering in the forests, and at night, hyenas annoyed them by howling unceasingly.[7]

Eighteenth-century European visitors commented approvingly on the neat rows of crops seen—potatoes, sugarcane, bananas, plantains, yams, peanuts, beans, manioc, cocoa palms, maize, millet, melons, lemons, pineapples, mangoes, oranges, indigo, and even cotton and coffee. And palm trees seemingly grew everywhere. At that time, farmers had many chickens, sheep, goats, and pigs, but after the early years of the eighteenth century, few cattle were seen, and more and more fields lay fallow. The villages visitors came upon were impressively orderly, and the villagers uniformly friendly. British Royal Navy Commander Frederick E. Forbes, also a fellow of the Royal Geographical Society and an opponent of slavery, who a year earlier had commanded a British warship that captured six slave ships, went to Abomey in 1849. After serving as British Vice-Consul in Whydah, he described his first glimpse of the interior of Dahomey.

> We walked through a beautiful undulating park-like country, studded with magnificent trees—sycamores 130 feet high, and the huge giant cotton with its enormous girt of root spreading over 40 square feet. The variety of flowers was remarkable, and, together with the brilliant and varied colours of the butterflies, rendered the scene at once fragrant and beautiful. No one that has not travelled in Dahomey will believe the beauty of its scenery. Africa is considered generally as "a wild expanse of lifeless sand and sky," and not supposed to offer so romantic and beautiful a country, where large clusters of grapes, rough in skin, but palatable in taste, grow on all sides.[8]

Most European visitors stopped at the clean and prosperous city of Cana (sometimes spelled "Kana") where the king maintained a large palace, although he spent most of his time in Abomey. A city six-miles square, Cana struck European visitors as "clean, neat and quiet," a seemingly regal place untouched by war, surrounded by cultivation so intensive that it "rivals that of the Chinese," and filled with thousands of birds with brilliant scarlet plumage.[9] The distance from Cana to Abomey was nine miles over a remarkably smooth road so wide that a British visitor wrote, perhaps with some exaggeration, that twelve carriages could travel along it side by side.[10] One visitor noted, however, that Africans routinely walked along it in single file, wearing a narrow rut in the road.[11] In both Cana and Abomey, European visitors were greatly restricted in their movements, usually being held under what many saw as a form of benevolent house arrest. They were well fed and cared for but were not free to do or see what they wished, although they were usually free to walk about under close supervision. As a result, although Dahomey was perhaps the most often visited kingdom in West Africa, it may have been the least well understood.[12]

Situated on a broad plain, at an elevation of 1,000 feet, Abomey was usually home to some 25,000 people, although one mid-nineteenth-century traveler estimated it at 50,000 to 60,000.[13] The king's principal palace there held as many as 7,000 to 8,000 people, almost all of them women. Abomey was not a walled city, but it was surrounded by a shallow moat that contained water only in the rainy season. By the late 1700s, the main entrance boasted over sixty cannon purchased through the slave trade but used only to fire salutes. Because there was no source of drinking water in the city, Abomey could not be defended for long in any event. Houses within the city were separated by empty spaces, where people planted all manner of crops, and although the city changed its appearance over the years—it was burned to the ground four times early in the eighteenth century—unlike Cana, it always impressed visitors as being shabby. Neither Cana nor Abomey could match the capitals of neighboring kingdoms for architectural elegance, hygiene, or sheer size. For example, Kumasi, capital of the Asante kingdom to the west of Dahomey, held many more people, boasted elegant two-story houses, and actually had flush toilets.[14]

The exception to Abomey's dismal appearance was the king's huge palace, surrounded by a twenty- to thirty-foot mud wall that stretched for well over two miles. It had a dozen entrances, each with a guardhouse. "Manning" these guard houses were richly uniformed, heavily armed women soldiers—the "Amazons."

The earliest European visitors to the Kingdom of Dahomey were surprised to find the king guarded by uniformed women armed with muskets, swords, and clubs. Noting the grim countenances and powerful muscles of these women—some of whom were over six feet tall—Europeans soon came to call them "Amazons," after the women warriors who the ancient Greeks insisted had fought so savagely against them. Later on, European visitors to Dahomey learned what the enemies of Dahomey already knew—these women were not only a supremely loyal corps of palace guards, but by early in the nineteenth century they were also elite professional soldiers, more disciplined, audacious, and courageous than Dahomey's best full-time male soldiers.

Before they were killed almost to the last woman by much better armed French troops in the early 1890s, for some 200 years Dahomey's "Amazons" had achieved a well-earned reputation for loyalty to their monarch, and during the nineteenth century they repeatedly displayed ferocity, bravery, and skill in battle. During the 1840s, they led Dahomey's army to several victories, including one in which its male soldiers fled under fire, forcing the Amazons to fight and win the battle alone. In 1851, and again in 1864, they valiantly stormed the walled city of Abeokuta, only to be shot down in large numbers, and although the bayonets and vastly superior firepower of French troops proved too much for the Amazons in 1892, their courage in battle against the French was unsurpassed, as many French officers and men were quick to admit. Dahomey was not the only African society to utilize women as palace guards or as warriors, but it was the most successful in doing so and was certainly the best-described example of women as professional, full-time soldiers anywhere in the non-Western world. And although women have fought bravely and well in armies in various parts of the world, nowhere else is there irrefutable evidence that they became the elite of their society's armed forces, a position they maintained in Dahomey for the better part of a century.

These women began as palace guards, a role reserved for women because no man was allowed inside the palace during the hours of darkness. If the king were to be protected at night, it had to be by women. But in addition, a succession of kings let it be known that celibate women, especially captives from other societies, were chosen as palace guards because they would most likely be free of ties to powerful Dahomean men or women who might try to conspire against the monarch. The Amazons protected their monarchs without fail over the course of two centuries. In 1818 some palace guards so faithfully defended the ruling king, d'Adandozan, against a palace coup that they died almost to the last woman trying to prevent his rival, Gezo, from toppling him. However, it appears that some other women soldiers fought for Gezo.[15] In what is an enduring mystery, although d'Adandozan was considered a despot, he was allowed to live in protected seclusion in the palace until he died a natural death in 1860, a fact suggesting that some loyal Amazons survived to protect him. He actually outlived Gezo.[16]

Although the Amazons apparently failed in their attempt to prevent d'Adandozan's overthrow, new king Gezo was so impressed by the courage and loyalty of these warrior women that he soon after recruited many more women soldiers, intentionally making them the elite corps of his army, as well as his palace guards. He gave them more elaborate, standardized uniforms, as well as many honors and rights that set them above male soldiers. If the Amazons had not been seen by all as Dahomey's elite troops in earlier times, they certainly were soon after Gezo took power. Their loyalty to all the kings who followed Gezo continued to be demonstrated beyond any question. Prior to this time, many of the women warriors, perhaps the majority, had been foreign slaves. After the coup d'état of 1818, King Gezo continued to recruit slaves from foreign kingdoms such as Yoruba into his palace guard and his female battalions, reasoning that these women would have no ties to his enemies within Dahomey. But Dahomean women were conscripted as well.[17] Chosen because they were large, strong, and sometimes cantankerous, these women were required to renounce all family loyalties during a dramatic induction ceremony after which they were declared "reborn," having broken all ties to their family and lineage, so that they were loyal only to the king.

Whether free or slave, women's entry into the army began with a blood oath. New recruits to the women's army were lined up before the veteran Amazons and their officers, where, after the recruits pledged their loyalty to the king alone, a priestess made an incision in each woman's left arm, catching her blood in a highly polished human skull. After the blood had been mixed with powder and alcohol, each recruit drank from the skull, an act that symbolically bound the women together as the priestess solemnly explained. They then swore never to betray one another. The women were also told that they were now invulnerable.[18]

It is not certain just when or to what extent the female palace guards of the early eighteenth century expanded their role to include service as soldiers during military campaigns. Dahomey oral history has it that women soldiers fought in a campaign as early as 1708, and others were said to have fought in the conquest of Whydah in 1727.[19] One visitor saw some 2,000 women parade in 1724, but they were probably royal wives, not warriors. A British visitor early in the eighteenth century was told that women had had to be recruited to help Dahomean men defend the kingdom at a time when the male army had been greatly depleted in battle. The women were told to dress like the men but stand behind them, giving the appearance of greater numbers to intimidate the enemy; when the enemy saw the unexpectedly large Dahomean army, they fled before the women could be asked to fight.[20] Throughout the eighteenth century, European visitors reported seeing uniformed women soldiers not only serving as guards for the king but as a separate part of the Dahomean standing army.[21] However, their numbers were never said to exceed 1,000.

After King Gezo reorganized his army beginning in 1818, making his women soldiers dominant and far more numerous, creating new battalions, and bestowing honors, the women became better drilled than the male soldiers both on parade and during campaigns, and these men were well disciplined themselves. Snelgrave gives this account of the male army on its return to Abomey in 1727 after conquering the Kingdom of Toffoe:

> In the afternoon, the Linguist [interpreter] came and told us, that the remainder of the Army, who had been plundering the Country of *Toffoe*, were returning; and asked us, whether we would go and see them pass by the King's Gate? We went accordingly to that place, and soon after they appeared, marching in a much more regular Order than I had ever seen before, even amongst the *Gold Coast Negroes*; who were always esteemed amongst the *Europeans* that used the coast of *Guinea*, the best Soldiers of all the *Blacks*. I observed, this Army consisted of about three thousand regular troops, attended by a rabble of ten thousand, at least, who carried Baggage, Provisions, dead Peoples Heads, etc. The several Companies of Soldiers had their proper Colours, and Officers, being armed with Musquets and cutting Swords; and with Shields. As they passed by the King's Gate, every Soldier prostrated himself, and kissed the Ground; then rose with such agility, as was very surprizing.
>
> I took notice, that [an] abundance of Boys followed the Soldiers, and carried their Shields; and asked the Linguist, "What was the occasion of it? He told me, That the King allowed every common Soldier a Boy at the publick charge, in order to be trained up in Hardships from their Youth: and that the greatest part of the present Army consisted of soldiers bred up in this manner, and under this Establishment." By which I judged it was no wonder the King had made so large Conquests, with such regular Troops, and his Policy together.[22]

Almost a century later, another British observer described Dahomean male soldiers on the march:

A day or two after this we had a view of a Dahomian army, consisting of five or six thousand men, who bivouacqued in the neighborhood of Grigwee: they were a wild looking group, and armed in the most irregular manner; some with musquets, others with swords, spears and clubs; they seemed, however, to be very orderly, and proceeded in good spirits, in chase of the foe, who had, by this time, retired towards their own borders, and as we afterwards learnt, the Dahomians took ample vengeance on the enemy's territory. [23]

Despite this praise for Dahomey's male troops, all European observers reported that the Amazons were even more impressive on parade and during campaigns than the men. In the mid-nineteenth century, British Royal Navy Commodore Eardley Wilmot, wrote, "They marched better than the men, and looked far more warlike in every way: their activity is astonishing."[24] Wilmot added, "Amazons are everything in this country . . . first in honor and importance."[25] When they fired their muskets at targets for Wilmot, he found their accuracy "astonishing."[26] Wilmot estimated the number of Amazons at 5,000, noting that there were many other women who acted as their servants and cooks.

Young girls thirteen or fourteen years of age were attached to each company, where they learned their duties but did not go to war with the company until they were more mature and could handle a musket. Wilmot wrote that these women were well aware of the authority they possessed, "which is seen in their bold and free manner, as well as by a certain swagger in their walk. Most of them are young, well-looking, and have not that ferocity in their expression of countenance which might be expected from their peculiar vocation."[27] Wilmot concluded of the Amazons, "They are far superior to the men in everything—in appearance, in dress, in figure, in activity, in their performances as soldiers, and in bravery."[28]

Amazons not only were seen on parade, in maneuvers, or guarding the king but sometimes also served as public executioners. For example, in 1889, when King Béhanzin took the throne, several hundred people were beheaded at his father's grave, including a dozen or so by Béhanzin himself. These were not only criminals or slaves taken in war but also members of the palace staff and many of the deceased king's wives, some of whom voluntarily took poison. Scores of war prisoners were tied up and carried in baskets before being carried around by Amazons as the crowd screamed for their death. At a signal, they were thrown to the ground to be, quite literally, torn to pieces. One Amazon beheaded a victim herself, then, as a French diplomat looked on in horror, licked the blood off her sword. Another executed two men.[29] Later, it appeared to some European visitors that many bodies were roasted and eaten.

The training of seemingly ordinary women to become capable of such acts began with their conscription. Women were subject to a different form of military induction than men. Beginning as one of King Gezo's reforms early in the nineteenth century, fathers were ordered to appear at the court once every three years with all of their daughters aged from as young as nine to fifteen or even older. The king and his ministers, assisted by high-ranking Amazons, selected the tallest and strongest of these girls for military duty. There were many tall, strong young women in Dahomey to choose from. Richard Burton went so far as to say that Dahomean women were taller and stronger than Dahomean men, who appeared "effeminate" to him and, he said, did no physical work.[30] Even slave parents presented their daughters, and those who were chosen for military service often became slaves to the free-born Amazon officers and were taken into battle to carry their weapons and gear.[31] Also conscripted were disobedient daughters.[32]

Those girls chosen for induction into the army were immediately made to swear an oath of chastity from which they could be released only by the king should he choose to have sexual relations with them. He freed others from this vow when the women approached middle age and left military service. All of these Amazons lived in barracks protected by the high mud walls of the king's palace compound and guarded by eunuchs sworn to protect their chastity, even though many of the new slave soldiers were not virgins and some had even given birth before being captured and conscripted into the army. It has been speculated that many were clitoridectomized to reduce their sexual desire, but there is no convincing evidence.[33]

What the Amazons did in public—on parade, during "customs," on campaign, and even during combat—was seen and reported by European observers and by French soldiers who fought against them, but very little is known about what they did when out of the public eye. Because European visitors were not allowed to penetrate the palace walls and because Amazons were not interviewed about their lives until well after Dahomey's army had been destroyed, we know little about how they spent their time. We do know that despite the renunciation of family ties, female kin could sometimes visit Dahomean Amazons, often bringing food with them, but slave soldiers had no kin in Dahomey, and presumably no visitors. It is likely that the Amazons passed their time chatting with one another and the king's wives, singing, dancing, exercising, or telling stories. We know that they wrestled and engaged in a kind of tug-of-war activity to increase their strength and combativeness. Physical training, including long marches, was frequent, perhaps even a daily occurrence.[34] They also made pottery and calabashes. It appears that their officers exercised stern control, and that slaves and younger Amazons served their superiors in many ways. Some Amazons may have established lesbian relationships, as Burton speculated, and as women did in Turkish harems, but we have no idea how they might have accomplished this under the watchful eyes of the eunuchs.[35] We do know that whatever these thousands of women warriors did behind palace walls somehow enabled them to maintain their physical conditioning, their remarkable morale, and their steadfast loyalty to their king.

And this was no mean achievement. Dahomean girls, like women captured from other societies, were raised to enhance their beauty, to increase their sexuality, and to be loyal to their parents and kin. Their goal in life was to become wives and mothers. The life of a commoner woman was not easy, but most women seemed contented enough to outsiders, many of whom, like Burton, had a very critical eye. When some of these young women became Amazons, all that they had been raised to live for had to be rejected. Whether slave soldiers or Dahomean women who were cut off from their families, Amazons were closely watched over by stern Amazon officers who insisted that they create new lives in which nothing mattered but loyalty, bravery, and military ability. Instead of enhancing their beauty as their mothers and sisters did, they hardened their nails in brine, then cut them to sharp points so they could be used as weapons.[36] They were also taught to walk with a masculine swagger. That thousands of women and girls could be remolded in this way is a tribute to the power of the Amazonian process of indoctrination, especially so, as the prospect of life as a soldier did not appeal to all young women. Some welcomed the call to military service, but others fled when recruiters came to their villages, and a few are said to have killed themselves.[37]

For these newly conscripted women soldiers, war honors would have to replace motherhood. Despite the rigors of their training—or perhaps because of it—young Amazons were made to feel not only special but superior in every way. With older Amazons as role models and continual praise from the king, most new women soldiers apparently not only accepted their military role but cherished it. A French visitor in the mid 1800s wrote that the king supported his Amazons "sumptuously" in his palaces and "they pass their time drinking, smoking and dancing."[38] Women soldiers who gave noteworthy service to the king were often rewarded with necklaces of beads or metal while truly exceptional service led to the public bestowal of honorific titles and gifts of valuables, including slaves. Exceptional Amazon officers received intricately carved wooden batons marking their rank and honor, silver-headed canes, gold-brocaded hats, even brass or silver-plated shields. Heroic women soldiers not only received many honors such as these, but the king often went out of his way to praise them to European visitors. King Gezo proudly introduced British Captain John Duncan to an Amazon officer who had captured a male prisoner in each of Dahomey's last two campaigns. Unlike the corpulent older Amazons Burton would describe two decades later, Duncan wrote that "Adadine is a tall thin woman, about twenty-two years of age, and good looking for a black, and mild and unassuming in appearance."[39] She knelt and humbly thanked Duncan repeatedly for doing her the honor of recording her name in his "book." In addition to individual honors, deserving units were rewarded with elegant battle flags, colorful umbrellas, ornate uniforms, and especially rum and tobacco, both of which the women soldiers are said to have consumed often and heavily.

Loyalty was rewarded, too. Tata Ajache was a slave woman who was raised as an Amazon. To honor her exploits in battle, she was given cowries and cloth by King Glele who later became so taken with her that they began a sexual relationship and she became pregnant. For some reason, the king asked her not to reveal that he was the father of her child. As her pregnancy became visible, Tata Ajache resisted beatings and all manner of coercion by Amazon officers without disclosing that the king was the father of her unborn child. Before she could be executed for her crime, King Glele rewarded her loyalty by giving her an honorific name celebrating her faithfulness and granting her elite status. He also gave her a house, two slaves, and baskets of cowries, beads, and cloth.[40]

Celibacy was made mandatory for Amazons not only to prevent pregnancy that would restrict a woman's ability to march and fight, but to prevent emotional ties to children or lovers that could distract a woman soldier from her total commitment to the king and military duty. The king nevertheless chose to take some attractive, still feminine young Amazons as sexual partners, and so did some young men who risked their lives to seduce them. Despite regularly taking an herbal concoction said to be a contraceptive, some Amazons joined Tata Ajache in becoming pregnant. While Sir Richard Burton was in Abomey, several pregnant women soldiers were tortured until they revealed the names of their lovers, then killed by other Amazons. The men who were named were killed, too, leading to the often-told joke in Dahomey that more male soldiers lost their lives climbing the walls of the king's palace than were killed in battle.[41] In this case, like most others, however, only a handful of men and women were executed for such an offense; the others were forced to serve in the army as part of an almost suicidal corps that led the army's charges. Known as the *gate-opening force*, these women led each attack and were usually the first ones to die.[42]

Once inducted into the army, new Amazons were subjected to a barrage of indoctrination to ensure their discipline and their loyalty to King Gezo, who was determined to create a military state led by his female soldiers. Each recruit was apprenticed to an older woman soldier who, as some surviving Amazons later said, subjected them to harsh discipline while they learned to crave the same kind of honors and prizes earned by older women warriors.[43] Later, after years of training, they attended numerous ceremonies dressed in their impressive military attire, where they again and again publicly pledged their devotion to the king. On one occasion in the 1840s, it took three hours for one battalion of 600 women soldiers to swear their loyalty to the king before he called out the names of particularly brave officers, who then knelt before him, covering themselves with dust, before running off at tremendous speed. They were led by a corps of drummers whose drums were decorated with human skulls and scalps.[44]

To underscore their devotion, Amazon battalions regularly danced with martial frenzy and frequently sang martial songs. A favorite song declared, "May thunder and lightning kill us if we break our oaths."[45] In another song, they declared, "Let us march in a virile manner; let us march boldly, like men."[46] Despite their masculine strivings, the Amazons could sometimes appear to be feminine. In the 1870s, an English visitor watched a company of women warriors dressed not in military uniforms but in elegant silk, velvet, and chintz, their bare breasts daubed with pale green pomade, dance demurely for two hours.[47] Despite ladylike moments like these, the Amazons were more likely to chant fiercely. One of their most common chants was this:

> *Lionesses are more fearsome than lions.*
> *Because she has her cubs to defend.*
> *And we, the Amazons, have you to defend.*
> *The king, our king and our God, ki-ni.*[48]

When it came time for war, they proved their loyalty to the monarchy time after time throughout the incessant wars of the nineteenth century. One striking example of their devotion came in

1851 after a failed attack on the Egba city of Abeokuta. One Amazon who had been taken prisoner proved to be an Egba herself, captured as a girl and raised in Dahomey. She refused to allow her Egba parents to free her, choosing to remain faithful to the Amazons, who eventually purchased her release.[49]

As they marched and danced in public, Amazons continually sang heroic songs such as one that included this line: "War is our pastime—it clothes, it feeds, it is all to us."[50] In another, they sang, "We will return with the intestines of the enemy."[51] In other songs, they promised to chop up their enemies like "mincemeat." When they were observed returning from battle actually displaying the scalps, genitals, and intestines of their enemies, Europeans were convinced that they meant what they said. In an impressive testimonial to gender stereotyping, the Amazons also chanted, again and again, that they had become men: "As the blacksmith takes an iron bar and by fire changes its fashion so have we changed our nature. We are no longer women, we are men."[52] On one such occasion, King Glele turned to Sir Richard Burton and muttered, "A woman is still a woman."[53] But the king took care not to be overheard by the Amazons. After an Amazon killed and disemboweled her first enemy, she was proud to be told by other women soldiers that she was a man.[54]

In one sense, the determination of the Amazons to be seen as men is paradoxical because male Dahomean soldiers sometimes fled from battle, earning the Amazons' scorn. For example, one of the Amazons' greatest victories came in 1849 against Atakpahm to the north. Although the male Dahomean troops panicked and ran away when the battle grew intense, the Amazons stood their ground, then attacked and routed the enemy. Later, they sang, "We marched against the Atahpahms as against men. We came and found them women."[55] Women soldiers came to deride their male counterparts who displayed cowardice by calling them "women." They had more than one occasion to do so because male soldiers were known to have fled from combat on several occasions, something that Amazons never did.[56]

Whether they had become men, were still women, or were some of both, the Amazons usually impressed onlookers with their masculine vigor. As a British army officer remarked, they made "a very imposing appearance, and are very active. From their constant exercise of body . . . they are capable of enduring much fatigue."[57] A few years later, in 1864, Burton saw little to please his eye as Amazons paraded past him on their way to war. He described them as "old, ugly and square-built frows" *(Fraus)*, who trudged "grumpily" along, amazing him with their "stupendous" buttocks.[58] If Burton exaggerated, as he was known to do, there is little doubt that at this period some Amazons were heavy women who were getting on in years. However, the women Burton saw were almost all killed in the failed assault on the city of Abeokuta a few months later.

The women who replaced them were young Dahomean conscripts often described as "charming," "graceful," and even "ravishing," even if, as some said, "barbaric."[59] A French observer in 1890 reported that the Amazons who would soon fight the French were as solidly muscled as Dahomean men and that some were old enough to have gray hair.[60] However, a photograph taken in this same year shows a score of young Amazons, all of whom were quite feminine and attractive in appearance, and during the Amazons' last campaign against the French in 1892, French soldiers often wrote about the beauty of some of the Amazons. The following is from a former British army officer, then serving in the French Foreign Legion:

> This dead Amazon was a very handsome and beautifully proportioned young woman, and her dead face bore a particularly mild and peaceful expression, utterly at variance with the bloodthirsty-looking machete in her girdle and the Winchester repeating carbine lying by her side. She had a very massive ring, made of particularly brassy-looking West African gold, on the second finger of her left hand. Not having any sentimental scruples about robbing a dead enemy, I took possession of this ring.[61]

Soon after their conscription, new women soldiers received training in the forest that would soon be put on display for European observers. The nature of this training no doubt changed over time, but it involved military, moral, physical, and religious instruction. Supervised by officers wearing coral necklaces and wielding small whips when needed, the new Amazons listened to endless admonitions about bravery and loyalty, swearing again and again "to conquer or die." While in the forest, they also learned to imitate the cries of birds as part of a secret language that was used to give orders during combat that their enemies could not understand.[62] The new Amazons were also taught to cope with hunger, thirst, and dangerous animals, as well as to treat wounds.[63] Again and again, they were taught to leap over the thornbush fences that enemies often erected as protective barriers, and to disregard the deep scratches they usually received. Throughout much of West Africa, larger cities were surrounded by high mud walls, but smaller ones and temporary military camps were protected by barricades of bushes containing two-inch-long, very sharp thorns. When properly emplaced, these fences could be almost as formidable as barbed wire. On special occasions, Amazons would display their prowess in coping with such barriers for the king and distinguished visitors. One such dignitary was John Duncan, formerly a British officer in the First Life Guards. After examining the eight-foot thorn barriers that had been assembled, Duncan wrote, "I could not persuade myself that any human being, without boots or shoes, would, under any circumstances, attempt to pass over so dangerous a collection of the most efficiently armed plants I had ever seen."[64] When the order to attack was given, the barefooted Amazons rushed the thorn barrier "with a speed beyond conception," and to Duncan's astonishment, in less than one minute the entire force had passed through it.[65]

Several Europeans witnessed demonstrations of Amazons in mock attacks and all praised their discipline. One wrote that the sham attack he witnessed in 1861 was carried out with "indescribable enthusiasm" as the women soldiers dashed through thornbush barriers and somehow climbed a fifteen-foot-high stockade.[66] Several European visitors reported witnessing Amazons rushing through thorn barriers and over high walls of fortresses to return to the king with the captives held within. These were sometimes slain on the spot, either by the king himself or by the Amazon who had retrieved the victim.[67] On another occasion, Forbes saw some 2,000 women soldiers form up into military formations before attacking a stockade constructed to represent an enemy fortification. The women were said to have attacked with amazing speed and precision. The one dissenter to these reports of the Amazons' dash and discipline was a British lion hunter who wrote a letter to the Duke of Wellington saying that the Amazons he saw in 1864 "maneuvered with the precision of a flock of sheep."[68] He may have been right, but the women he saw were new recruits who had replaced the experienced Amazons killed a few months earlier at Abeokuta.

The year after Forbes had watched the Amazons' mock attack, King Gezo staged a public display of his entire army for the edification of several European visitors, including French official Auguste Bouët, who described what he saw: "On a vast plain outside of Abomey, the entire professional army of men and women, all richly uniformed and armed for battle, was drawn up outside a palisaded village that had been built for the spectacle that was to follow. Inside the village, many slaves, including women, yelled in mock defiance."[69] The king placed himself in the center of his army surrounded by five or six thousand Amazons, with the male soldiers forming the wings of the huge formation. At the king's order, a group of Amazons, camouflaged with long grass, crawled toward the village, firing their muskets while lying prone. Bouët reported that the villagers returned a "very heavy fire," but he did not indicate whether real bullets were exchanged.[70]

Following another order by the king, more Amazons sprinted forward and climbed the palisade, followed by other units of women who joined the attack, capturing all the "enemy" and setting fire to the village. Amid victorious shouts, they returned with their prisoners and with carved wooden heads representing victims hanging from the ends of their muskets. Bouët wrote ecstatically about the discipline of the Amazons, their efficiency, and the coordination of the attack, which to him duplicated that of a European force complete with scouts, reserves, buglers, drums, and messengers.[71]

It was soon after this martial display that Dahomey's army, led by its women soldiers, failed in its attack on the fortified Egba city of Abeokuta, suffering terrible losses. Despite this defeat and the heavy loss of life among the Amazons, five years later two other French visitors were similarly impressed by the Dahomean women warriors as they simulated another attack, immediately following one previously carried out by Dahomey's male soldiers. A French naval officer reported that the women soldiers had outdone their male counterparts in their passion and fervor. "One would have said [it was] an army of demons spewed up by a volcano."[72] Répin agreed, writing that the women attacked with animation and fury:

> It's difficult to describe, even to imagine, the picture they presented, under a fiery sky, amid the swirl of dust and smoke, the crackling of musketry and the roar of cannons, these four thousand panting women, intoxicated by powder and smoke, moving convulsively with the contorted faces of the damned and uttering the most savage cries. Finally, when all was exhausted, the ammunition and the energies, order and silence were restored.[73]

Young Amazons were also well trained in the use of their weapons, principally muskets, using adulterated powder and bits of iron in place of bullets; short swords that resembled machetes; and, in the early eighteenth century, bows and poisoned arrows. They also wielded eighteen-inch-long razors that folded into wooden handles and were released by a spring. These latter weapons, each weighing about twenty pounds, were invented by one of King Gezo's brothers for the Amazons' use.[74] They were also taught to use their fingernails and teeth as weapons, something they did very well, to the great distress of the French in the 1890s. Because hand-to-hand combat was their specialty, they smeared their arms, legs, and breasts with palm oil so that an enemy could not maintain a grip on them. European observers reported that they not only drilled well but engaged in target practice and shot their muskets accurately.[75] They always handled their muskets with military precision, but by the time of their first war with France in 1890, their aim with musket fire was often poor. However, without bullets that fitted the barrels and with no wadding to compress the powder and prevent it from spilling out, and firing while at a dead run toward their enemies, that is no surprise. Even so, their fire was often lethal. Whenever a Dahomean soldier killed an enemy, the soldier had the right to glue a cowrie shell to his or her musket stock with a paste of dried blood. Some musket stocks of older women warriors were completely covered with cowries.[76]

Burton reported that the Amazons fired their muskets from their shoulders, unlike the male soldiers, who fired from the hip to avoid recoil, and that they could reload faster than men. Foa concurred, writing that Dahomean women could complete the seven movements needed to reload a musket in thirty seconds compared to fifty seconds for men.[77] However, in 1892, when they fought the French a second time, some of the Amazons had been issued newly purchased American Winchester repeating rifles. Their fire from these weapons was usually inaccurate because the Amazons often fired these weapons held hip high as they charged forward. However, some women who stopped to take aim, or who fired from a trench, did so with deadly accuracy.

It is doubtful that the Amazons did anything comparable to the marching drills of European armies; if so, they did not display this practice in battle. However, they did display great discipline when they marched in review before their king.[78] On campaign, the Amazons were organized in three wings. Women in the right and left wings typically wore blue-and-white-striped tunics over short pants, but uniforms varied from time to time and unit to unit. The right wing always outranked the left, but the center corps, composed of the king's palace guards, was the elite of the Amazon army.

Each corps had a distinctive hairdo. The Amazons' headgear varied over the years, but palace guards consistently wore their distinctive white cotton, bowl-shaped hats with a blue crocodile sewn on each side. Later, some Amazon units wore red fezzes, each with an eagle feather, and others wore what resembled red nightcaps. Each corps was made up of women with different kinds of weapons. There were also famous elephant hunters, prized markswomen who regularly hunted elephants to provide ivory for the king, and who served as sharpshooters during battle. Several Europeans saw evidence of their success as hunters when these Amazons presented ivory tusks to the king in the Europeans' presence.[79] Some of these women became effective snipers against the French. Other Amazons were armed only with their long razors used to cut up the dead, usually taking their genitals, scalps, and intestines as trophies. It was said that sometimes victims were cooked and eaten, but no European appears actually to have witnessed this.

Most women soldiers carried a musket, a short sword, a knife, or wooden club in a waistband, which also held a sack of powder, a cartridge pouch, and a length of rope to tie prisoners. Muskets were very well taken care of with frequent cleaning, and both the firing mechanism and the muzzle were covered with leather to keep them dry.[80] Nevertheless, many muskets were defective. If blacksmiths were not available to repair them, they were heated and pounded into swords. During the eighteenth century and the early part of the nineteenth century, the youngest Amazons carried bows and poisoned arrows, but these were abandoned when more muskets became available. Each woman had a leg tattoo (usually a crocodile) that extended from waist to knee, wore an ivory bracelet on her left wrist, and was bare-breasted in battle. Some newly enlisted and as yet untrained women served as porters and also carried away the wounded after a battle.[81]

Estimates of how many Amazons served at any point in history varied. At some times, estimates ran as high as 8,000, the number Duncan insisted he saw in the 1840s. In the early eighteenth century, when they served primarily as palace guards, they may have numbered only a few hundred, with no one claiming to have seen more than 800. Later in the eighteenth century, visitors reported seeing around 1,000 Amazons. Throughout most of the nineteenth century, there were reported to be 3,000 to 5,000 uniformed women warriors.

Before the king mobilized the militia for a campaign, the Amazons would carry out martial displays near his palace.

> There were bayonetresses, with blue cloth tunics, and a white patch on the shoulder, white fillets like those of the men, sashes to match supporting their swords, and variously-coloured pagnes. The blunderbuss women, distinguished themselves by scarlet woolen nightcaps. After they had danced and sung . . . all raised their weapons steadily, with left arms extended, and fired from the shoulders, not from the hips as the men do to avoid the kick; they returned with a kind of caper, and they did not flinch after the fashion of the Dahoman (male) soldiers.[82]

When a large military campaign was being planned, headmen of villages were ordered to send a certain number of men to Abomey to be issued government gunpowder before going to war. These militiamen would join the regular soldiers, both male and female, who were continually on duty. Each male and female soldier was expected to return with at least one prisoner or the head of an enemy, or risk a penalty. Although Dahomey's early campaigns were wars of conquest and annexation, as years passed it appeared to European observers that the wars these Dahomeans fought were intended only to destroy neighboring societies and capture slaves. The Dahomeans vehemently denied this, insisting that they were primarily driving their enemies away and, secondarily, securing captives to be sacrificed during their "customs," a practice that was widely known in the region. It is true that some enemies had to be driven away and that slaves were needed for sacrifices, but many more slaves were sold or put to work on Dahomean plantations than were ever sacrificed.

When a newly mobilized Dahomean army assembled in Abomey, it first underwent religious, protective rituals; then it was greeted by florid, hyperbolic speeches delivered by various Amazon officers. These promised great victories, terrible losses for the enemy, and wonderful honors and rewards. King Gezo's response could be stern to say the least:

The hunter buys a dog, and, having trained him, he takes him out a-hunting, without telling him the game he expects to meet. When in the bush he sees a beast, and, by his teaching, the dog pursues it. If the dog returns without the game, the huntsman, in his anger, kills him, and leaves his carcass as prey to the wolves and vultures. If I order you to clear the bush, and you do not do it, will I not punish you? If I tell my people to put their hands in the fire, they must do it. When you go to war, if you are taken prisoners, you will be sacrificed, and your bodies become food for wolves and vultures.[83]

Gezo meant to be taken seriously, and he was: "His Dahoman majesty, King Gezo, is about forty-eight years of age, good looking, with nothing of the negro feature, his complexion wanting several shades of being black; his appearance commanding, and his countenance intellectual, though stern in the extreme. That he is proud there can be no doubt, for he treads the earth as if it were honored by its burden."[84] The call for actual war was made by the king declaring that "his house wanted thatch," which "alludes to the custom of placing the heads of the enemy killed in battle, or any of the prisoners of distinction on the roof of the guard houses at the gates of his palaces."[85]

Well before these ceremonies took place, "spies" said to possess great supernatural power had been dispatched to the enemy's territory to weaken their religious protection and magically spread discord among the population. They also mapped the territory, its towns, their defenses, and the homes of prominent people to be captured or killed. When the army actually marched, this magician-spy had his hands bound and was made to march at the head of the army. If the Dahomeans were ambushed, he was instantly killed, but if the war went well, he was given land and slaves.[86] Other spies were sent out to pose as traders, and they, too, were relied on to bring back useful information. Finally, when the army marched toward the target of its attack, it took circuitous routes, sometimes even marching well past its enemy's territory before doubling back to launch a surprise attack.

The officers had their food and weapons carried for them by small slave girls, and the common soldiers carried packs on cradles that contained their bedmats, clothes, and food for a week or two, most of it being toasted grain and bean cake, seasoned with peppers. There were cartridge pouches around their waists, and slung over their shoulders were "watergourds, fetish-sacks, bullet-wallets, powder-calabashes, fans, little cutlasses, wooden pipe-cases enveloped in leather tobacco-bags, flint, steel, and tinder, and Lilliputian stools, with three or four legs, cut out of single blocks."[87]

On some campaigns, the king accompanied his army, often riding a horse and surrounded by his women soldiers. When the army halted, a mat enclosure was constructed for him and the Amazons. The royal quarters, distinguished by their superior size, were placed beyond the danger of ambush. The soldiers camped promiscuously in little huts or slept on the ground, the men separated from the women by the mat fencing. The army moved at all hours, frequently at night, sometimes guided by captives kidnapped from the place about to be plundered. A few soldiers, dressed as traders carrying cloth and tobacco, preceded the force collecting valuable information. The army itself advanced by circuitous routes, cutting its own roads through the bush. False reports were spread about its intended direction. Extreme caution was ordered when the army was close to the destination. No talking was allowed, and even smoking was forbidden for fear of betraying the army's position. The point of attack was secretly reconnoitered by a chosen spy during the day. Dahomean troops surrounded the targeted village so cautiously that it was often taken by surprise, as they assaulted before dawn, with a wild rush, uttering piercing screams. The only village defense was usually a fence of thornbushes, and these the Amazons easily brushed aside. As a rule, the object of such a campaign was to capture, not to kill. Only the old, the sick, and others of no value as slaves lost their lives. The others were tied and marched back to Abomey, where the king purchased them.

Any chief who was captured was reserved for public sacrifice during the annual "customs" in Abomey.

What it was like to be captured by a force of Amazons was recalled by a man who was captured and sold into slavery in the United States in 1859. One morning at dawn, as he and fellow villagers in the Kingdom of Tokkoi were beginning to stir, Dahomean soldiers led by Amazons were suddenly everywhere, beheading those who fought back with a single sword's blow. He tearfully recalled his own attempts to escape, pointing out that although he had been nineteen at the time, the Amazons "were too strong for me." He was tied and marched back to Abomey with other captives. Some, like the king of Tokkoi, were beheaded by Amazons, their bodies left to rot while their heads were smoked over a fire and taken back to Abomey.[88]

As we have already seen, a victorious army returned to Abomey or to Cana to the wild acclaim of the populace—muskets were discharged, Amazons danced and sang in triumph, the king offered praise, and the crowds were delirious with joy. Dahomean losses were not discussed, and the Dahomean wounded, who were almost always helped back, were kept out of sight. What happened after the return of a defeated army has not been recorded, but it is likely that the monarchy never publicly admitted defeat.

2

The Kingdom of Dahomey

The Kingdom of Dahomey came into being as the result of a dispute within the ruling family of a small kingdom named Allada sometime during the first half of the seventeenth century. The losers of the contest decamped, moving northeast to Abomey, where they began to create their new vision of monarchy while conquering nearby small chiefdoms. Unlike the people of Allada and all related peoples, including the populous and powerful Yoruba, whose semidivine kings ruled only with powerful checks and balances, these newly established Dahomeans believed that their king should not be divine but should possess an aura of absolute authority. Moreover, for reasons not known, they decided that this authority should be backed by the force of a standing army, something that was unknown in the region even among much larger kingdoms like the Yoruba to the east and the Asante to the west, both of which would later go to war with Dahomey.

Inside their palaces, surrounded by their many wives and some eunuchs, and always closely guarded by Amazons, a succession of kings ruled as what European visitors believed to be absolute, tyrannical monarchs. For example, John M'Leod, the British surgeon who visited in 1803, wrote, "It is a monarchy the most unlimited and uncontroled [sic] on the face of the earth."[1] If this had been true, it would have been a striking departure from the forms of monarchy known among nearby kingdoms closely related by language, culture, and history, where kings were very much under the control of nobles, the royal lineage, and families of wealth. But even though most visitors, later including the distinguished anthropologist, Melville J. Herskovits, declared Dahomey's king an absolute monarch, he was hardly that. However, he and his court created the appearance of his absolute power with extraordinary success.[2]

Dahomey's first known king, Dako, reigned from perhaps 1620 to 1640 or 1650. He was followed by King Wegbaja, after whom this early period is usually known. Following his death around 1680, Dahomey's leaders strengthened this vision of absolute monarchy so well that when Agaja became king in 1708, he was able to complete the transformation of Dahomey into a state where the sovereign appeared to rule without question, women soldiers defended him vigilantly, and a full-time, professional army backed his every decision. Fortunately for the newly founded kingdom, Agaja was a man of great ability. Well known to French, Dutch, Portuguese, and British visitors, Agaja was described as a highly intelligent, farsighted man who could be generous, even magnanimous, with enemies, and who had a keen sense of humor but an iron will.[3] One admiring French visitor rapturously described him as of middle height, "slightly bigger and having wider shoulders than Molière," the famous seventeenth-century French actor and writer of comedies.[4]

A few years after his accession to power, Agaja's troops defeated Allada and soon after conquered most of the related kingdoms on the coast, including the Kingdom of Whydah in 1727, taking control of its valuable port.[5] This victory, in which 5,000 Whydah people were killed and 10,000 captured, came about with great ease, primarily because the people of Whydah were not eager to fight, and perhaps also because Whydah had very little gunpowder. Legend has it that the king of Whydah's wife was Agaja's daughter, and at his request, she soaked all the powder in the Whydah armory the night before the attack.[6] It is unlikely that this too simple explanation was the true cause of the Whydah collapse, but whatever the actual reasons, Agaja next ordered that all of the European slave-trading posts be destroyed and that forty white men be captured and held for fifteen days before being released unhurt, but well chastened by Agaja's display of power. Agaja's acts have been interpreted as evidence that he opposed the slave trade. It is far more likely that he was attempting to gain direct control over it.[7]

Most Europeans believed that Dahomey, like other African kingdoms, fought primarily to capture slaves, who could be exchanged for European goods, especially guns and gunpowder. Because Dahomey could not survive without guns and gunpowder and because it had nothing else to trade except slaves, Agaja's attempt to control the trade was understandable to European slave traders. But the Dahomean monarchy's reasons for war were more complex than this. Some years later, Lionel Abson, director of a British trading company on the coast, asked a subsequent Dahomean king about the reasons why Dahomey went to war:

> In the name of my ancestors and myself I aver, that no Dahoman man ever embarked in war merely for the sake of procuring wherewithal to purchase your commodities. . . . If white men chuse [sic] to remain at home, and no longer visit this country, will black men cease to make war? By no means. . . . God made war for all the world, and every kingdom, large and small, has practiced it more or less.[8]

After the conquest of Whydah and the surrounding coastal region, Agaja's newly established kingdom of Dahomey covered less than 13,000 square miles, an area about the size of Rhode Island. In comparison, the neighboring kingdom of Asante held some 3 million people occupying a territory the size of Wyoming. At its height in the early nineteenth century, Dahomey probably held no more than 250,000 people, and later it became so noticeably depopulated by wars that visitors wondered where the inhabitants had gone. In the mid-nineteenth century, one British observer reckoned that the population could not have exceeded 180,000, three-fourths of whom were women and children, the men either off to war, killed in previous ones, or shipped overseas as slaves.[9] But at the height of Agaja's reign, the kingdom was densely populated with bustling, industrious people whose energy impressed European visitors who had characterized the Africans they had previously seen elsewhere as lazy.

Throughout his reign, Agaja increased the strength of his kingdom and his army by incorporating war prisoners into his society as slaves. By the mid-nineteenth century, one European visitor estimated that 90 percent of Dahomey's population were slaves, most of them Yoruba, only 10 percent being free people born in Dahomey.[10] This seemingly dangerous ratio of slaves to free men could not have been as unbalanced during Agaja's early reign, when the slave trade was new, but his kingdom nevertheless included numbers of slaves. Now that his kingdom controlled the important slave-trading center of Whydah, his adamant refusal to support the Oyo-dominated slave trade with European traders enraged leaders of the Oyo kingdom, a much larger, more powerful populace to the northeast who wanted to trade slaves to Europeans at the coast. Needless to say, this refusal also infuriated the European traders. The Yoruba-speaking Oyo not only had a much larger army than Dahomey but also had thousands of cavalrymen, something Dahomey could not hope to match because Dahomey was in the southern tse-tse fly zone, where horses did not long survive fly-borne trypanosomiasis.

The Oyo not only defeated Dahomey but also forced Agaja to support their slave trade and to pay annual tribute. Whenever the Dahomean king annoyed them, another Oyo army of horsemen would sweep down on Abomey and burn it to the ground, forcing the king and his court to take refuge in a dense forest hideaway twenty-five miles away to the northwest. On one such flight, the king took a British trader named Gregory with him, but Gregory apparently left no record of his experiences.[11] The inhabitants of Cana and many smaller towns also fled, once escaping only by leaving so much brandy behind that the Oyo troops were said to have become too drunk to fight.[12] Oyo invasions took place four times between 1726 and 1730, greatly disrupting Dahomey's econ-

omy and destroying its military power. Surprisingly, no one betrayed Agaja when he went into hiding, and the Oyo never captured him.

In between Oyo attacks, Agaja continued to rule Dahomey with
a combination of charm and ruthlessness. One of the first
Europeans to write about his visit to Abomey during Agaja's reign
was William Snelgrave, a British Royal Navy captain engaged in
the slave trade, who visited in 1727. Before meeting King Agaja,
Snelgrave and his well-armed party were almost smothered by
Dahomeans eager to see and touch the white men. After spending
five hours with the king, Snelgrave left this impression of him:

> He was middle-sized, and full bodied; and, as near as I could judge,
> about forty-five years old: His face was pitted with small pox; never-
> theless, there was something in his countenance very taking, and
> withal majestic.[13]

But Snelgrave was under no illusions about the king's tough-
ness. When the British governor at Whydah, a man named Charles
Testefol (sometimes written "Testesole"), insulted Agaja by sup-
porting the king of Whydah, then ordered a high-ranking
Dahomean official to be flogged, the king ordered Testefol's death.
His order was carried out when several Dahomeans captured the
Englishman, staking him to the ground on his stomach before
making numerous cuts on his arms, back, and legs. These cuts
were filled with a mixture of lime juice, salt, and pepper, causing
Testefol excruciating pain for some hours before he was beheaded.
Snelgrave was convinced that Testefol was then eaten, citing two
Portuguese slave traders who quoted the Dahomean executioners
as saying, "That English beef was very good."[14] Six years later, a
Dutch delegation was being warmly received by King Agaja, who
danced with them in a generous welcome. Favorably impressed,
they described him as elegantly dressed but quite portly.[15]

When Agaja died in 1740, his successor faced a broken economy,
a reduced share of the slave trade, and the seemingly implacable
hostility of his Oyo overlords. The youngest of Agaja's four sons

was chosen to succeed him, largely, it seems, because he had spent years as a hostage of the Oyo, knew many of their nobles, and, most important, knew how to deal with them. Taking the title of Tegbesu, he set his sights on cooperating with the Oyo in making Whydah the supreme slave-trading center in the area. Before he could achieve that, however, he had to reestablish his "absolute" authority. This was problematic because two of his brothers had contested him for the throne. Along with many other people in West Africa, Dahomeans insisted that royal blood could never be shed, so Tegbesu ordered his older brother (who had apparently not been named king because he had earlier fled in a crucial battle against the Oyo) sewn up in a hammock and thrown into the sea. All of this brother's accomplices in his bid for the throne were executed or sold into slavery. Tegbesu also placed a curse on his other disloyal brother and all others who might challenge his authority.

Tegbesu proved to be formidable, to say the very least. He had his father's intelligence, and he was ruthless to a degree his father never matched. European observers thought him a despot, and he did execute many people whom he disliked, including army officers who had become too popular or who had lost a battle. He also clarified the rules of succession, creating the precedent that before his death the king would name one of his sons as successor.[16] Fourteen years later, Tegbesu tested the willingness of his subjects to accept this new rule of succession by conspiring with a few of his royal wives to be declared dead. For six months, he disappeared with some wives and women palace guards while his son "succeeded" him. When it became clear that there would be no challenge to the new king, Tegbesu reappeared and resumed his rule, to the astonishment of European observers and, no doubt, most Dahomeans.[17] When one British visitor met him in 1766, he appeared to be "about seventy. His person was rather tall, he was graceful in his manners, and very polite to strangers, though the dread and terror of his own subjects."[18]

Soon after Tegbesu became king, he turned Whydah into a highly organized, thriving slave port. Dahomeans served in a large army garrison there, and others worked as messengers, water carriers, porters, canoemen, storekeepers, laborers, washerwomen, prison guards, and police spies. All received a standardized wage set by the king, who often personally oversaw details of the slave trade. At a time when a man could eat well on 3 to 5 cowries a day, some at Whydah earned 2,000 cowries a day, and many received 100 or so.[19] The slave trade was so profitable that in 1743, Tegbesu was able to give such a lavish gift to the Oyo that he was allowed to return to his principal palace in Abomey. The slave trade continued to flourish as rising prices for prime slaves, high customs duties, and lavish gifts from British, Dutch, French, and Portuguese slavers made Tegbesu's kingdom so prosperous that he erected seven regal palaces, and the common people also prospered. By 1776, Dahomey was wealthy, but to ensure peace, Tegbesu still had to pay an annual tribute to the Oyo, and the Oyo could veto any use he might wish to make of Dahomey's army. The Oyo also limited the perceived majesty of Tegbesu by denying him the right to wear "regal" clothing such as silk damask.[20]

Still Dahomey's prosperity continued. When Robert Norris, another British naval officer and a slave trader, visited Abomey in 1772, he became the only European to be allowed inside the king's bedroom when the sovereign was too ill to see him elsewhere. After walking to his door along a path that was completely paved with the skulls of war victims, Norris entered a circular room, well-appointed with European furniture and containing many expensive silver cups, plates, and other items of considerable value.[21] Although shocked by the skulls, Norris was impressed by the king's wealth. David Mills, former British governor at Cape Coast Castle to the west, visited Dahomey five years later. Unlike Norris, Mills opposed the slave trade, but he was also much taken by the wealth that he saw and by the kindness of the people:

The natives both male and female are the most civil, good kind people I ever saw, full of compliments and as quick and tame as you possibly can imagine. . . . The country appears amazingly populous, and they appear happy, contented and cheerful.[22]

Mills was so taken by the decency of the common people of Dahomey that he seriously considered settling in a Dahomean village but finally concluded that his family considerations made that impossible.

This prosperity and contentment were in some considerable measure a result of the slave trade that brought in not only wealth but the muskets and gunpowder that allowed Dahomean armies to capture still more war prisoners to use as farm laborers or sell as slaves. But they also derived from the well-organized centralized governmental control that gave the common people of Dahomey comfortable, meaningful lives. In principle, the king owned all property, although he rarely confiscated it except in cases of criminal conduct. Similarly, he also had supreme powers to collect taxes, tolls, and tribute; decide all matters of policy; set the prices of goods in the markets, which he also owned; impose a sales tax on sellers; standardize the currency; declare war; and even decide what crops should be planted.[23]

In reality, with the advice of his *kpojito,* or "queen mother," and others, he appointed the best government officials he could, and they controlled virtually all of these matters. To the amazement of European visitors, who expected African societies to be chaotic, the kingdom was without famine or paupers, and there was very little crime. The practice of publicly beheading criminals was meant to be a deterrent to crime, as was the spectacle of salting a dead criminal before exhibiting his body atop a twenty-foot-tall pole in a public square for months at a time, but such practices were common in West Africa, and some kingdoms remained riddled by crime.[24]

To maintain this orderly social world—called by one historian, "the most advanced form of political organization in Africa"[25]— the king appointed numerous ministers with lofty titles to take charge of such matters as foreign affairs, collecting taxes, safeguarding the treasury, imprisoning and executing criminals, commanding the secret police, overseeing the king's slaves, commanding the army, and supervising markets and agriculture. Most of these bureaucrats lived and worked in the capital city of

Abomey, where the king's huge walled palace held his thousands of wives, who were watched closely by more than 100 eunuch attendants led by a chief eunuch, who had powerful influence over the king and court. Other ministers lived in Cana and even smaller towns. But they did not live in the royal palaces. The everyday rule over the kingdom's countryside was in the hands of provincial governors, who could, when necessary, call upon the army for assistance. Overall control of the countryside was apparently delegated to a viceroy, known to Europeans at the time as the "bush king."[26] Dahomey's markets were government-controlled, and the police maintained excellent order in them. In Abomey, there was a nine o'clock curfew enforced by patrols of torch-bearing armed police.[27]

Dahomey also created institutions that gave meaning and predictability to peoples' lives, while maintaining a criminal justice system that successfully controlled crime. For example, because the king and numerous wealthy men possessed so many wives, there were too few unmarried women for younger men, and the resulting threat of conflict as these young men pursued older men's wives was a serious one. To control adultery and the problems it could create, the king commissioned and paid a large corps of royal prostitutes to serve the sexual needs of men at low cost. For example, in the mid-nineteenth century the price of a royal prostitute was only 20 cowries, whereas a chicken cost 280 cowries.[28] Despite their low wages, these prostitutes paid taxes. The court also sold female slaves as wives at low cost to low-ranking Dahomean men who were thought to be deserving.

As noted earlier, European visitors to the kingdom of Abomey routinely reported that the king was an absolute monarch, an impression that each king was at great pains to reinforce. Later, serious scholars reached the same conclusion. As mentioned earlier, American anthropologist M. J. Herskovits did so, and similarly, French historian Edouard Foa concluded:

> The Dahomean form of government is an uncontrolled, absolute monarchy without limitations. This permits all sorts of abuses on the

part of the king. His smallest caprice is a law to which all his subjects, from the highest to the lowest, must submit without murmur-
ing. And he changes the statutes at the whim of his fancy. Far from
accepting the wise counsel which those surrounding him are able to
give because of their age and experience, the sovereign listens only
to his own desires.[29]

But Sir Richard Burton saw through the king's pretense of absolute power, writing that "collectively, [his ministers, war captains, and priests] are too strong for him, and without their cor-
dial cooperation he would soon cease to reign."[30] Recently,
modern scholars have raised serious doubts about the king's
power, and one, John C. Yoder, has shown compellingly that
Dahomean kings were far from being arbitrary autocrats.[31] He
has demonstrated that they were shrewd politicians who ruled
by appealing to the complicated and competing needs of various
coalitions. For one thing, kings never appointed their royal kinsmen to positions of power for fear of creating competitors for the
throne.[32] In modern times, princes and princesses are still mis-
trusted. As a commoner said, "Royalty is capable of anything.
They can never be trusted."[33]

Reexamining the writings of various European visitors, especially F. E. Forbes, who wrote in extensive detail about the
Dahomean political process, Yoder showed that by the middle of
the nineteenth century, and no doubt earlier as well, Dahomey's
dreaded annual ceremony known as the "customs" was not simply the religious ceremony it was thought to be by European visitors, but an annual political meeting similar to that of a Western
legislative council.[34] Each year at the time of this ceremony, dignitaries from all over the kingdom were required to attend. In all
their finery, accompanied by armed retainers, they arrived in
Abomey to take part in what was known as the Great Council. For
several weeks some 300 delegates from all parts of the country de-
bated and decided issues of national importance. The delegates included the highest-ranking ministers, leaders of the royal lineage,
high-ranking wives, and even wealthy Brazilian slave traders,

some of whom had enormous influence, but there were also middle-level officials, army officers, village chiefs, tax collectors, and famous soldiers of both sexes, especially Amazons.

This annual ceremony began with all the ritual grandeur that we examine further in the next chapter, but in 1850, when Forbes witnessed the events after the grand ceremonies had been concluded in about ten days, during the next two weeks or so the king met with important officials, and the Great Council held legislative sessions focused on diplomacy, defense, economic priorities, and military planning as well as the promotion and demotion of officials. The politicking that continued throughout this time took place during almost every free moment, especially during evenings. Instead of smoke-filled rooms, prominent Dahomean delegates set up their stools and colorful umbrellas in the open air, where they did in fact smoke their pipes while they greeted well-wishers and listened to their complaints and requests for favors.[35]

The sessions of the Great Council were intense and candid. Forbes recorded one incident in which the minister of commerce *(Meu),* the second highest official in Dahomey, was "sharply" rebuked by a low-ranking army officer. When the minister responded by physically assaulting the officer, the king sharply chastised his minister and supported the officer.[36] The king listened to most of the debates and publicly voiced the council's final consensus, but it was clear that in any serious matter he could not act without the support of the council. In fact, a strong case has been made that by the mid-nineteenth century, and perhaps earlier, actual political parties existed that greatly influenced Dahomean politics.[37] The king had power that was often exhibited in public arenas, but he was more often an arbiter between powerful interests than a policymaker on his own. For the government to function, it was important that the king appear to possess absolute power, but as in most West African kingdoms, in reality the king's "absolute" powers were constrained by the powerful families and royal kinsmen who had put him in power, as well as by ministers, army officers, priests, and even wealthy slave traders. His powers were also limited by prominent women.

Like some of their neighbors, including the Oyo, the Dahomean people believed in a dual cosmology that balanced the living and the dead, right and left, royal and common, and most important—and far more so than other West Africans—they believed in a universe that was half male and half female. Only if the two genders were united in harmony could life on earth avoid disaster. At least by the time of King Gezo's rise to power in 1818, and probably earlier, the people of Dahomey put this principle into practice by appointing for each male official a female counterpart, known as his *kpojito,* or "mother." These women were given the responsibility of knowing everything that the official said or did and reporting immediately to the king and his closest confidantes anything that might be of interest.

Unlike the Dahomean male officials, the "mothers" lived in the king's palace, where they had ready access to him. No man was allowed in the palace after sunset, so the king was left alone with his women and their eunuchs. And anything a man wished to say to the king during the day had to be whispered first to an old woman, who passed the message along to the king, sometimes altering its meaning if she chose to. Selected women also attended all of the king's meetings with his counselors, and even the king himself was symbolically—and, in some respects, actually—subordinate to his "queen mother." Intrigue was rampant, but because women in the palace controlled the flow of information to the king, and because they were usually intensely loyal to him, many men lived in great fear of them.[38]

Most men were ambivalent about women, loving, hating, fearing, respecting and sometimes deriding them.[39] But duality, or "doubling," was so basic to the people of Dahomey that even the chief eunuch had a female double, and the Dahomean people loved twin babies, a rarity among the world's societies; in many of them, one twin was put to death.[40] In fact, in Dahomey, twins were treated more reverently than other children. They were always dressed alike, and gifts to one had to be duplicated for the other. If one died, a small wooden image was made and the surviving twin carried it at all times.[41] Because the first gods were said to have given birth to twins, a twin birth was considered ideal, and a cult of twins with elaborate feasts and rituals played an important role in Dahomean life.[42]

Due largely to "doubling," few societies in Africa, or elsewhere for that matter, achieved as much social unity under the direction of a monarch as Dahomey. Even so, Dahomean kings lived in morbid fear of coups. Even King Agaja, who inspired great loyalty from his people, lived in dread of a palace coup.[43] His successor, Tegbesu, was even more fearful, and later monarchs continued to suspect palace coups, sometimes with very good reason. For example, in 1797, King Agonglo responded to Portuguese pressure that in return for expanded trade he would convert to Catholicism by agreeing to undertake Catholic instruction, which would be followed by baptism. How serious he might have been about this will never be known because the threat of such a change in Dahomey's religion was so shocking to members of the royal lineage that a prince named Dogan organized opposition in the court. When Portuguese priests returned to begin Agonglo's religious instruction, they were sent away after being told that the king had "smallpox," probably a metaphor used to signal that a monarch was in disfavor rather than a literal description of a physical illness.[44]

Soon after, a woman in the palace named Na Wanjile, who expected to be appointed queen mother by Dogan, either shot or poisoned Agonglo, and dynastic combat followed. Even though Prince Dogan arrived at the palace with over 300 armed men the morning after Agonglo's death, he lost the power struggle.[45] Agonglo's second son was installed as king because his oldest son had a physical defect.[46] The new king, supported by the army and most government ministers, ordered that Dogan and Na Wanjile be buried alive, and many others who had opposed Agonglo were executed or sold into slavery. Before slaves such as Agontime boarded ships at Whydah, they were branded on the shoulder or the chest. In a modest gesture to gentility, women were not branded as deeply as men because they were said to be more "tender," a form of compassion not common in the slave trade.[47] One of those sold into New World slavery was Agontime, the *kpojito* of future king Gezo who would take power through another coup in 1818.[48] A powerful priest, she apparently spent twenty-four years in Brazilian slavery before a Dahomean royal deputation located her and returned her to Abomey. The name she chose after her return, Agontime, meant "the monkey has come from the country of the whites and is now in a field of pineapples."[49]

In an effort to reduce the danger of a coup, secret societies—numerous and important in many parts of West Africa—were banned in Dahomey, and large numbers of secret police unobtrusively watched everyone for any sign of crime or danger to the king, as did the king's wives and the armed women who constantly guarded him. Special messengers stood ready to convey information rapidly to any of the provincial chiefs or influential European traders. Known as *half-heads* because they shaved one half of their heads, while the hair on the other half grew very long, they also wore long strands of human teeth draped over one shoulder. The teeth were supposed to be those of enemies or criminals personally killed. The half-heads engendered obvious respect. When sent with a royal message, a half-head ran at full speed until he came to a prearranged relay post and another took over.[50] If necessary, half-heads could easily carry a message from Abomey to Whydah in a single day, a distance of sixty miles. In addition to their attempts to control information, kings sometimes came to rely on the support of powerful slave traders. King Gezo owed the success of his coup in 1818 in large measure to the support of the wealthiest slave trader in Dahomey, Afro-Brazilian Francisco Félix de Souza. For years after Gezo came to power, de Souza's wealth, wisdom, political astuteness, and charm served the king so well that when he died, Gezo gave him a royal funeral complete with the sacrifice of a boy and a girl, who were buried with him to attend to his needs in the next world.[51]

When someone was arrested for a crime such as rape, adultery, theft, arson, or murder, the accused was ideally to be judged only by the king. More often, however, the case was adjudicated by the prime minister, the *migan*, who could impose the death penalty, although that, too, was supposed to be a power held only by the king. Not all criminals were killed, however, as many received a sentence of life imprisonment, being sent to work on a slave plantation on the River Cuofo so dreadful that it was named "Let no one set their foot there." Here they were compelled to work in the king's fields for the rest of their lives unless pardoned.[52] Sometimes, there was more novel punishment. One official thought guilty of malfeasance was ordered not to bathe, shave, or cut his fingernails for several months, during which time he was required to sit each day outside a palace gate, humbly available for public inspection.[53] Another man who drank too much was forced to sit in the same place while quite drunk day after day while passersby mocked him. Law and order were well served in Dahomey, but the king was never without an escort of armed women soldiers, and secret police were very nearly everywhere. Europeans were warned to be very careful about what they said to one another no matter what language they used. One was warned, "If you want to chat, go into open fields and even then beware!"[54]

As we have seen, some Dahomean women, like some slave women, became full-time soldiers, and some other women became prominent in the exciting affairs of the court, but most Dahomean women, whether slave or free, lived more humdrum lives, not much different from those of women in most nearby societies. They collected firewood, drew water from distant streams, weeded fields, tended crops, and harvested. The work was hard, and common women were usually much more active than men. In addition to farmwork, women also wove baskets, made pottery, and sold goods, including food they cooked and carried to markets. Women also had primary responsibility for child care and for feeding their families. Men were free to have multiple wives, whereas women could have only one husband, and at marriage—or even earlier— had to move into their designated husband's family compound. Women were also forced into seclusion during menstruation, and men sometimes openly scorned them. The most wounding insult that could be inflicted on a man was to say, "He is less than a woman."[55] Wives also acted submissively around their husbands, at least when Europeans were present.[56] As we have seen, this status and behavior changed when a woman became a soldier.

In some ways, however, Dahomean women were far more privileged than most other African women or, for that matter, most women known to human history. First, a wife had the socially recognized right to divorce her husband, but a husband was not permitted to divorce his wife. What is more, each woman had the right to reject any husband proposed for her whom she did not favor. Wives were free to keep whatever they earned by their sales in the markets, and they also controlled whatever inheritance might come to them.[57] In another example of remarkable female privilege, women in the royal lineage were free to take any man they wished as a lover, including married men, and they often did so, much to the distress of many commoners.[58] This was permitted despite Dahomean laws that made adultery for nonroyals a serious, even capital, crime. However, royal men had no such privilege, as only the king among royal men had similar license to choose any woman he wished.[59] Priestesses of religious cults also had a right to sexual license, a right they often exercised. They also had considerable political power over the king.[60] And in what may have been an attempt to enhance the lives of older women, when teenaged boys finally healed after circumcision, they were required to have sexual relations with a widow or a postmenopausal woman before they could seek out any girl of their choice.[61]

Within the Simboji Palace in Abomey, there often were between 5,000 and 7,000 women, all considered *ahosi,* royal "followers" or "wives." Many were armed Amazons, only a few of whom had sexual relations with the king (although an unknown number had clandestine sex with other men). Still, most kings appear to have had sex with hundreds and perhaps thousands of *ahosi* even though they fathered relatively few children. King Glele, who ruled for thirty-one years, left only 129 children, although King Béhanzin, who ruled for only four years, left 77.[62] Many *ahosi,* like Amazons, were slaves, but others were gifts from prominent families seeking to curry favor with the king by presenting him with their beautiful young daughters as yet other wives.

The palace was the center of power in Dahomey, and the king's *ahosi* had enormous influence over the use of that power. For these women, the palace was a "city within a city," complete with its own market for the use of women only. Not only did the king's women control access to the king, but at least some women were also always present when the king granted a visitor a "private" audience. And every visitor was assigned a royal wife as his "mother," someone who arranged for his needs to be met while keeping him under continual and careful surveillance. Women also helped to shape public policy, supervised public meetings, and achieved power on their own. A group of eight women was always present when the king met with his counselors.[63] Nevertheless, not all slave women found palace life palatable, and some chose to escape. A European trader witnessed the execution of five slave women who had escaped to their homeland, only to be returned to Abomey by a king loyal to Dahomey. Other *ahosi* who refused to conform or achieved too much power could be sacrificed during annual ceremonies.

Most of the king's wives worked in his palaces by cooking, working at crafts such as textiles and pottery, or making uniforms for the army, while the affairs of state swirled around them. Some of these women dressed plainly, but the highest-ranking wives personified elegance,

> each under her own state umbrella of gorgeous hue. They were dressed in green and blue silk, richly embroidered with gold lace, and glittered in the sun in the profusion of their jewellery of silver and coral. All wore a string of silver ornaments round their heads, which contrasted well with their dark skins, and the royal coiffure of a turban-like tuft on the top of the head was combed and pomatumed [whitened] to perfection. Each carried a fish-slice sword; and on arriving before the king they were presented with a tumbler of spice on a silver salver [tray].[64]

Women like these who managed to call the king's attention to themselves could receive royal titles along with gifts of land and

slaves, including the right to sell their slaves at Whydah. These titles and property could later be inherited by female relatives in the
woman's lineage, a group of kin who traced their descent from a
common ancestor. In this way, or by becoming madams of houses
of prostitution at Whydah, some Dahomean women became so
wealthy that they successfully founded new lineages, of which
they were the heads. Yet, abuse of privilege, even elitism, per-
vaded the palace to such an extent that foreigners could not help
noticing it. There was also an intense atmosphere of intrigue, as
ambitious and talented women vied for prestige and power.[65]
Neither Dahomeans nor foreigners could hope to achieve their
goals without the support of some well-placed women, and all
men feared angering them.[66] So did other women, because some
women were not above falsely accusing a rival or an enemy of
adultery or other crimes.[67]

A Frenchman held prisoner for three months in Abomey in 1890
saw some court life during the last few years of Dahomey's existence as a sovereign kingdom. He wrote this:

> The king's women play a considerable part in the politics of the
> country; they attend council meetings, their opinions have great
> weight with the king. They are the ones who refresh his memory on
> certain facts and prompt him on his addresses or speeches to the
> chiefs and to the people.[68]

Several decades earlier, a visiting missionary reported that
women, including Amazon officers, presided over judicial appeals
in which their opinions not only were taken seriously but were
"ascendant."[69]

Women achieved great power as "doubles" for high officials including the *migan,* or prime minister, whom his female double
could actually overrule.[70] But the highest rank to which a woman
could aspire was that of "queen mother," a term that translated as
"she who places the leopard on earth," referring to the totemic animal ancestor of the royal lineage. This woman was rarely if ever
the natural mother of the king.[71] Not only did the king and his

queen mother rule in some senses jointly, but both appear to have campaigned for their offices.[72] All of the queen mothers came from frontier regions that Dahomean kings were attempting to integrate more fully into Dahomey, a fact suggesting strongly that these women were high-ranking war prisoners. Bay reports that despite their foreign birth, these women often amassed greater wealth than the brothers or sisters of the king, and some continued to wield great influence even after the death of their king.[73]

Far removed from the excitement, glitter, and intrigue of the king's court, most Dahomeans lived their lives in highly ordered, even regimented, routines that governed their fields, markets, and homes. They did so cheerfully enough and worked with such industry that foreign visitors very often commented on it. William Bosman, the Dutch slave trader, was the first European to record his visit to the coast at Whydah:

> Whereas on the Gold Coast Negroes indulge themselves in idleness, . . . here, on the contrary, Men as well as Women are so vigorously industrious and laborious, that they never desist till they have finished their Undertakings.[74]

Europeans made similar references to the hard work habits of both men and women in their fields, at their iron forges, and in their markets over the next two centuries. Boys and girls were taught to embrace this ethic of hard work at a very young age. Common women were expected to work hard in their fields, to walk great distances to and from markets to sell their goods, to cook well, and to see to the needs of their children. Men did not work as hard as women, but they did do physical labor, and it was often said that every man had to know, at the very least, "how to cut a field, how to build a wall, and how to roof a house."[75] Despite their hard work in the heat, Dahomeans impressed Europeans with their cleanliness, a result of their frequent use of soap made locally from palm oil and potash.[76]

At the end of the dry season, when the earth was almost rock hard, men began the task of hoeing to break up the soil. Sometimes, trees and brush had to be removed and burned. As with roofing and many other tasks, this work was almost always done by a group of three or four men exchanging cooperative labor. Once the field had been cleared and turned over, its owner had to determine how best to encourage the aid of the supernatural beings known to watch over new land. To do so, he would visit a diviner who performed various ceremonies. If the response was favorable, the farmer went alone to his field, where he used some soil to mold a human head with cowrie shells for eyes, placed it on the ground, then offered it palm oil and maize mixed with the blood of a chicken, flour, and water. The diviner later determined the name of the guardian spirit whom this head was meant to propitiate, and the farmer made regular offerings to this and other spirits thought to reside in trees. Only then could crops be planted. The same procedures were followed in Abomey and Cana, where considerable open farmland stood available between houses.

Once the crops were planted, their care became women's work, and between trips to the markets, women worked hard to weed and cultivate the land, while children drove away birds. An agricultural cycle was rigidly adhered to, based principally on rainfall. By August, all crops had been harvested, except millet and cotton, which required another month to grow. A new set of crops was planted in September leading to a second harvest in December. Harvesting was done by women, often in cooperative groups, who turned it into a festive occasion with songs, feasting, and numerous ceremonies in which various supernatural entities were thanked. One of these ceremonies, the Yam Festival, lasted four days with only women taking an active part. The dry season of January and February was devoted almost exclusively to hunting.

Except when occasional invasions of locusts took place, food was usually plentiful, and although maintaining the fields required hard work, Dahomeans abstained from agricultural work on numerous days each lunar month lest the thunder gods be offended and kill people. Palm trees were extremely common in Dahomey, making palm oil a profitable crop and an easy one to produce, as little care of the trees was required. The palm tree had such religious significance that every Dahomean of whatever social class had to own at least that one palm tree under which his umbilical cord was buried.[77] Because Dahomean officials prohibited drunkenness, the making of palm wine for local consumption was unlawful within the kingdom, but the sale of palm oil overseas began to replace the slave trade in the mid-nineteenth century. The making of palm oil was also primarily women's work.[78]

Raising animals was far less important than agriculture. There were few cattle, and their milk was not usually prized. Sheep and goats were eaten, whereas pork was a delicacy. All three animals often found themselves offered in sacrifices to various gods, as did chickens, which existed in large numbers. Ducks, guinea hens, and turkeys were available, too, but in smaller numbers. Hunting played an even more significant role than animal husbandry. As mentioned earlier, during the two dry months of every year, agriculture ceased, and hunting replaced it. Each village had a group of specialized men who did the hunting under the supervision of a hunting chief, who was responsible for taxing them. The hunting took place primarily in the tropical rain forests, where men's experiences were charged with supernatural meaning. There was obvious danger from carnivores, such as leopards, and another kind of danger from apparently harmless animals like antelope. A hunter who killed an antelope could neither speak, eat, nor drink water until he had reported to his hunting chief and a ceremony for the animal had been performed.[79] Despite ritual proscriptions like these, food from the hunt played an important part in the Dahomean diet. Honey was considered a delicacy, too, but it was supposed to be reserved for use by the army on campaigns.

Dahomeans honored their weavers and ironworkers as well as their hunters and farmers. Weavers produced handsome cloth from cotton, raffia, and the two combined. Ironworkers tended to be localized in separate villages or quarters of larger towns, where they produced and repaired a host of weapons, tools, and ceremonial objects such as gongs. Both of these occupations were exclusive to men. Pottery making, on the other hand, was exclusively the work of women. In addition to large storage jars, women made bowls and small pots for everyday use as well as ceremonial pottery for the serpent cult, which will be discussed later. There were also artists of both genders who worked principally in gold, silver, and brass. Much of their work was fine by any standard. They also made designs for ritual cloths and ceremonial umbrellas, and carved wood and calabashes. Some of the statuettes they carved were destined to adorn temples; other, more mundane items included furniture, gourds, and mortars and pestles.

As Dahomeans went about their everyday tasks, their dress varied considerably. Small girls seldom wore anything but a string of beads around their hips; small boys often wore nothing at all. Before both sexes reached puberty, they wore a cloth tied around the waist that covered their loins, but young women continued to leave their breasts bare. For common people, standards of dress changed little over the years, the usual costume for the workday being a cloth tied around the waist, although older women sometimes pulled it up to cover one or both breasts. On more special occasions, men would also wear a cloth tied over one shoulder. City women, and especially the king's wives, wore more elegant dresses, sometimes augmented by handkerchiefs, headpieces, and rings of silver on their fingers, with beads and cowrie shells around their arms and ankles.[80] With the exception of the king, a few of his close relatives, and a very few dignitaries, no one was allowed to wear sandals, not even army officers, chiefs, counselors, or high ministers.

Dahomey was a cash economy with prices rigorously set and enforced by the government, the value of the cowrie carefully maintained at 32,000 to an ounce of gold, or 2,000 cowries to a dollar. Forbes complained that he had to hire five women to carry fifty dollars' worth of cowries to Abomey. But this was a time when a dollar would buy 400 eggs or 2,000 oranges.[81] The concept of property was highly developed. In principle, as mentioned earlier, everything of value ultimately belonged to the king, but in reality some families acquired enormous wealth in land, slaves, money, and precious metals, whereas most of the kingdom's people lived at the subsistence level. Some property, such as groves of palm trees and land held for ancestral shrines, was held in common by members of a lineage. However, magic charms for protection or to ensure success in hunting were private property.

Men were known to borrow money in times of need, and sometimes repayment could not be made at the agreed-upon time. To extend the time before payment came due, the borrower could offer one of his children to the lender as a pawn, a transaction witnessed by the village chief and others.[82] Pawned children, usually girls, were made to work but were otherwise well treated.

Property was acquired through hard work, something children learned very young as they helped their parents in the fields. They also made little fields for themselves, where they grew crops they gave to the women in the family to sell in the markets. Little girls were permitted to sell their own valuables—salt, a few pieces of sugar, fried yams—or to cook food for their mothers to sell. All market prices were set, and there could be no bargaining. Anyone who attempted to haggle could be beaten by market women and even arrested by market police.[83] Valuables displayed in markets were protected with the full force of law, and there was a religious aura, too, as rituals were held in markets and at times bards recited sacred tales from Dahomean history in them as well.[84]

An example of how seriously destruction of property, and perhaps its desecration, could be taken comes from an event Robert Norris witnessed while en route to Abomey in 1772. The viceroy, whom Norris had met previously, asked to speak to him before his departure from a town halfway from the coast to the capital. When Norris arrived, "I found him passing sentence of death on a criminal, a middle aged woman, who was on her knees before him, in the midst of a circle formed by his attendants."[85] Norris asked that she be spared, offering to buy her as a slave. Thinking that the viceroy would grant this request due to their previous acquaintance, Norris was surprised to be told that the king had personally passed the sentence, decreeing that her head should be cut off and impaled on the stake lying next to her that she had been required to carry all the way from Abomey:

During this conversation a little girl, prompted by curiosity, and ignorant of what was doing [sic], made her way through the crowd; and discovering her mother, ran to her with joy to congratulate her on her return. The poor woman, after a short embrace, said, "Go away, child, this is no place for you," and she was immediately conveyed away.[86]

As a crowd of spectators listened, and the woman picked her teeth with a straw from the ground "with seeming indifference," the viceroy announced the sentence, reminding everyone that the king demanded obedience, submission, and orderly behavior. One of the executioners then clubbed the woman on the head, and as she lay on the ground, her head was severed and mounted on a pole to be placed in the marketplace.

It seems that this woman had kept a shop in a local market, where, a few days earlier, she had discovered that some "trifle" had been stolen from her. She had taken a burning stick from a nearby fire and, waving it over her head ("a usual custom in the country"), shouted, "Whoever has taken my property, if they do not return it, I wish they may die and be extinguished like this stick."[87] A spark from her blazing stick had accidentally fallen on the dry thatch of one of the huts, setting the market on fire, and destroying everyone's property.

Even more important than the entrepreneurial skills and hard work needed to acquire property were the social skills and moral values necessary to be chosen as the child who was to receive a family inheritance. Although there was a tendency toward primogeniture, families could decide which one of their children, including girls in some instances, should inherit. This decision was formalized by either a man or a woman's telling his or her "best friend"—a formal role recognized throughout the kingdom—how his or her property should be inherited. After death, this best friend announced these wishes to the survivors, who appear rarely to have disputed the decree. A father often made this decision early in life, quietly letting the heir know about it, and maybe only later becoming so disheartened by the boy's behavior that he would choose another heir. To spare the original heir public shame, the father would make no announcement of his choice before his death, often creating lasting bitterness and hostility when the "best friend" declared that someone else was to be the heir. An heir could even inherit his father's wives, except for his own biological mother.[88] As can readily be imagined, when a man possessed great wealth, including several wives and many slaves, the tensions among his potential heirs could be explosive. The process of inheritance was the same when a woman died, but because fewer women possessed great wealth, their choice of an heir appears to have generated less concern.

Inheritance helped to create a leisure class in Dahomey consisting of men and women who wielded considerable influence and owned slaves but engaged in no productive labor themselves. These people supported the king, the court, the priests, and the diviners, and they contributed to ceremonies. They also raised militiamen in times of mobilization. Beneath these wealthy, privileged people were free farmers, artisans, and market women. There were also slaves born in Dahomey, who could not be sold outside the kingdom and might, in some cases, eventually achieve wealth and power. Finally, there were many foreign-born slaves, usually taken in warfare, who could be made to work long hours and could be treated harshly, sold to traders, or even sacrificed. Unlike many other African societies, in which slaves became members of the owner's family and could eventually lose their slave status altogether, Dahomean slavery was seldom benign. Most slaves worked on royal plantations under conditions so harsh they were similar to those in the New World. In 1850, Forbes described one Dahomean who owned over 1,000 slaves: "as deep a villain as ever breathed."[89] He went on to note that members of the leisure class were ill advised to display wealth ostentatiously unless the king approved:

> If he brings more soil under cultivation, or in any manner advances his family to riches, without the license of the king, he not only endangers his fortune, but his own life and the lives of his family; in-

stead of becoming a man of property and head of a family, he is condemned to slavery.[90]

This was a threat intended to emphasize the king's power, and
wealthy men of intelligence were at pains to provide valuable gifts
and services to the king and other notables.

Still, the temptation toward rapid upward mobility clearly remained, as it does in many money economies. The government
brought this potentially disruptive temptation under control by collecting heavy duties on trade goods, including slaves, and by imposing a rigorously supervised system of taxation that was managed by the women of the king's court. Taxes were heavy and the
collection process rigorous. Customs collectors were stationed at all
markets, at all public roads, and on each side of Whydah. There
was also a very heavy head tax on slaves, which appeared to fluctu-
ate on a sliding scale based on the owner's wealth. Thanks to the
continual supervision of male tax agents by women in the palace,
nothing of value escaped taxation, and corruption appears to have
been avoided. An elaborate system of information gathering
guided the hunting chiefs, who taxed hunters, and farming chiefs,
who carefully determined the value of crops to be taxed.
Agricultural taxes were paid in kind—for example, the tax on palm
oil was one-third—and used to provision the army.[91] Livestock was
counted in various ways and taxed as well. In an important innova-
tion, the king had his own fields taxed in the same proportion as
that paid by every Dahomean. The result was an image of fairness.
This tax income was needed to support the king's court, his wives,
his army, and the government, but as we shall see in the next chapter, much of the king's wealth collected in these ways was returned
to the people during the annual "customs" ceremony, and many
deserving individuals received gifts throughout the year as well.

Ordinary life in Dahomey, like that in most parts of West Africa,
centered on the home, where each wife and her children lived; the
compound, which was a walled enclosure containing the households of each of a man's several wives; and the community, consisting of several compounds, sometimes surrounded by a thorn

fence or a low wall. Because foreign visitors were confined to their living quarters in Cana and Abomey, they saw little of village life. As a result, much of what is known about the details of everyday life must be inferred from the writings of French officials and scholars in postconquest Dahomey, the research of American anthropologist Melville Herskovits, who visited Dahomey in 1931, and the more recent reconstructions of various historians.

There is little doubt that membership in kinship groups, particularly the lineage, was a powerful unifying force, as it was among most neighboring peoples. It still was central when Herskovits was there in 1931, and the lineage had actually been weakened by that time.[92] Before French conquest, it is known that each patrilineal lineage had a chief, and that old women of the lineage also had authority, as well as both secular and religious responsibilities. For common people no less than royalty, it is likely that one's lineage membership played a large role in all aspects of everyday life. It was directly concerned with maintaining proper relations with the ancestors, a vital matter for Dahomeans, as what must be done and what must not be done with regard to them was critical. Each lineage had a distinctive name and food taboos, some of them involving the totem animals from which lineages were said to have been descended.

Few details of the influence of lineage membership on everyday life can be confirmed prior to the French conquest, but it is certain that the worship of lineage ancestors had to be faithfully carried out. Even though Dahomeans of earlier times, like those of more modern ones, lived life fully in the here-and-now, the need to ensure continuity of life after death led men and women alike to carry out the most intricate religious ceremonies honoring their ancestors. And these ceremonies were equally necessary to protect lineage members throughout their lives on earth. The importance of shrines was shown by their universality, for no compound was complete without a building where its ancestral dead were worshiped and rituals in their honor were carried out. Except for the members of two lineages that mysteriously did not deify their ancestors but worshiped only the sky gods, all Dahomeans participated in the cult of the dead. For some, the worship of ancestors may have been the only form of religious affiliation; for example, royal princes may not have been members of other religious cult groups:

> Whether of royal blood or commoner, however, the importance of the ancestral cult is paramount. In the life of every Dahomean, his ancestors stand between him and the gods who personify the forces of the universe that periodically threaten him with destruction. As an integral part of social organisation, on the one hand, and of religious expression, on the other, the respect and worship of the ancestors may then be thought of as one of the great unifying forces that, for the Dahomean, give meaning and logic to life.[93]

There were also numerous mutual-aid societies in Dahomey, including ones exclusive to women. Such societies pooled their money to help members when a need arose, and some of the women's societies were richer than those of men. These groups had special songs to be sung in public, accompanied by gongs and rattles. During King Glele's reign, some husbands of these women complained to the king that their wives should be at home in productive work, not engaging in such public performances. In response, there was a public meeting, after which the king ruled that women had the right to belong to as many mutual-aid groups as they wished. It would appear that some well-placed women had the king's ear, as usual.

After the birth of a child, most mothers abstained from work outside the home for six months to a year. Even the wife of the poorest husband stayed home for three months, and during this time, other women provided her with food, firewood, and water. Until the age of seven or eight, when children began to work with their parents in the fields chasing away birds or selling small items in markets, both sexes played together during the day and then gathered in the evening to tell stories or pose riddles that the others had to solve. At around the age of ten, boys no longer slept in their mother's house; instead, several boys built their own house and slept there together. As the boys approached puberty, their talk turned often to sex. At the same age, girls still slept at the houses of their mothers or grandmothers. At puberty, girls begin their preparation for sexual relationships through instruction by older women in the art of enlarging the vaginal labia by irritating them with a stinging plant or applying stinging ants to them, and then in response to the irritation and pain, pinching and pulling the labia until they eventually enlarged and elongated. Boys, on the other hand, began their preparation for sexual relations by following adults' advice to watch goats and dogs in action. To the surprise of Europeans, who thought all Africans sexually precocious, most Dahomean adolescents knew little about sex, and many had no sexual intercourse before marriage.[94]

No ceremony marked puberty for boys, but girls' first menstruation was recognized in a modest ceremony. In early puberty, both sexes sometimes developed homosexual relationships, but if these persisted into adulthood, they had to be hidden. At the age of around fifteen, boys had one or two of their upper incisors removed, and they were circumcised between the ages of seventeen and nineteen, again with little ceremony. Teenaged girls—along with a few boys—underwent cicatrization on the face and various parts of the body. The process was very painful, but the resulting keloids were thought to be beautiful and erotic, especially those on the lower back and inside the thighs of women, areas men caressed during sexual encounters.

There were two forms of marriage. In one form, valuables were given to the bride's father and the groom received legal control of the children. In the second, no valuables changed hands, and any resulting children remained in the lineage of the mother, more evidence of women's relative equality in Dahomey. All marriages involved solemn pledges followed by feasting and dancing. The newlywed couple could not have intercourse for three or four days, but after this period of sexual abstinence, consummation finally took place and more lavish festivities were held. All brides dressed in their best finery, and for royal brides, this included jewelry, as the following account by a British visitor indicates:

We found the new wife got up in splendid style. She was apparently about eighteen years of age, by no means bad looking, and profusely decorated with jewelry. Coral and silver necklaces and bracelets covered her neck and arms, and round her head she wore a fillet of black velvet, from which a number of silver and gold coins descended, after the fashion of the Fellah girls in Egypt.[95]

Married life was seldom tranquil, especially when a man had more than one wife. Cowives rarely became fond of one another, as this song, which they sang about one another, demonstrates:

> *Woman, thy soul is misshapen*
> *In haste was it made, in haste;*
> *So fleshless a face speaks, telling*
> *Thy soul was formed without care.*
> *The ancestral clay for thy making*
> *Was molded in haste, in haste.*
> *A thing of no beauty are thou,*
> *Thy face unsuited for a face,*
> *Thy feet unsuited for feet.*[96]

The children of cowives were also competitive and hostile, leading to frequent disputes among cowives and annoyance on the part of their husband. If a husband became sufficiently distressed by a wife's conduct or that of her children, he had to find a way to encourage her to divorce him, as he could not divorce her. If she resisted, he might beat her or openly insult her parents, hoping to bring about the desired end. Despite tensions among cowives and the actuality of divorce in some cases, most marriages seem to have endured, and foreign visitors often remarked that both Dahomean men and women appeared to be content.

With old age came great respect, not only because of the knowledge older people possessed but because they were thought to be close to the ancestors, whom they would soon join in the afterlife. Grandparents were especially favored as they cared for their grandchildren, played with them, and told them stories, all of which both the children and the older people greatly enjoyed. Older people also enjoyed their relative leisure and the opportunity to visit friends. Dahomeans of all ages had a zest for life and a fear of death, but death was seen by all as the beginning of a new existence in which they would rejoin their ancestors. When death came, typically after a long vigil by children as well as adults, it triggered one of the most dramatic rituals in Dahomean culture.

First, the women of the compound began to wail, soon joined by the men and children. After some time, the "best friend" of the deceased managed to stop the wailing, and the family began to wash the corpse with a native sponge and warm soapy water. The body was then shaved to remove all hair, and both fingernails and toenails were clipped. All these were wrapped in a cloth to be buried later with the body. A deathwatch followed, and the body was never alone until the time came to dress it for burial. Even then, burial was anything but routine. Digging the grave proved to be a costly and highly ceremonial undertaking, followed by a period of perhaps seven days when the body was only partially interred. Before the final interment took place, relatives filled the grave with all manner of things thought necessary in the next world. Many speeches followed, complete with dozens of testimonials and even more declarations of good intentions, before members of the deceased's cooperative work group assembled to sing songs in praise of the dead person. The body was then carried about the compound by loved ones from evening until daybreak while all sang the praises of the deceased, declaring their good wishes.

Eventually, the grave digger appeared, and while family members ate and danced, testimonials were recited at great length, presents were provided for the deceased, and the body was finally buried. A period of mourning followed marked by many ritual requirements. All this was well understood and even rehearsed, but should a child die while its parents were still alive, the burial ritual was slight because it was thought unnatural for children to die before their parents did. Whether child or adult, the funeral was not only a means of ensuring an appropriate transition to the next world but also a way of demonstrating, through lavish display, that other Dahomeans recognized the wealth, piety, and good character of the bereaved.

Dahomean religion had much in common with that of neighboring peoples, particularly the Yoruba, from whom many ideas had been borrowed even before the nineteenth century, when many newly captured Yoruba slaves brought living versions of their cults, diviners, and priesthood with them. A man was thought to have four souls; a woman or child had three. These souls sometimes left the body, later to return. At death, the souls accompanied the corporeal body to another world. The dead were believed to reside in the sky, it was said, because efforts to locate them in the earth or the ocean had always failed. To reach the world of the ancestors, the newly deceased person had to cross several rivers by paying a boatman. Some Dahomeans believed that there were also mountains to climb. Little was known about the lives of the ancestors in the next world except that they were thought to be joined by members of their families and their lineage, and to be attended to by slaves. It was known that the world was created by a female god, Nana-Bauka (or Buluku), who gave birth to twins. A shrine to the creator existed in a sacred village, where many people made pilgrimages to worship her. One of the creator's twin children was Mawu, a female god who reigned at night. She was cool, allowing people to sleep and refresh themselves. Mawu was revered, whereas her twin brother, Lisa, who reigned during the day, was "sun, heat, labour, all hard things."[97] When there was an eclipse of the moon or the sun, it was said that these two gods were having sexual intercourse.

Whether during eclipses or not, these two sky gods begat fourteen children, who in turn gave birth to still more children, all of whom became sky gods of greater or lesser importance. Some were worshiped by priests, who established shrines, organized cults, carried out sacred rituals, and initiated new members into the esoteric world of that particular god. Dahomean kings tried to make these cults subordinate to the monarchy, but with only partial success. Some cults had power that overshadowed that of the monarch who tried, but invariably failed, to control them.[98]

Believers brought food and other valuables to cult shrines hoping to be blessed or at least to avoid danger.

The power of cult priests and priestesses was a major constraining force on the authority of the king. There were also earth and sea gods, many of which could be highly dangerous. The thunder god made people and fields fertile but would also punish criminals, often after being urged to do so by outraged priests. Sea gods could be deadly, too, and one earth god visited smallpox on people who offended deities or violated secular laws. There was also a snake cult in Dahomey that intrigued foreign visitors, but it paled in comparison with the Kingdom of Whydah's serpent-focused religion, which gave snakes a central place in its pantheon. In 1727, a British visitor to Whydah named Smith saw a snake on the path and was about to kill it when his companion, the British governor, saved the snake, saying to Smith that if he had killed it, he would have been killed in return.[99] Another visitor reported that an Englishman who actually killed such a snake was later murdered. In Dahomey, the worship of some small, nonpoisonous snakes did take place, but it was peripheral to the lives of most people.

The divine trickster, Legba, was anything but peripheral; his presence was central to Dahomean theology. Throughout the kingdom, people erected temples to him, filled cult houses with believers, carried out private rituals, made offerings, and conducted public ceremonies, some of them riotously obscene. In one, a young woman tied a large wooden phallus around her hips. As she danced toward her audience of women, she caressed the phallus erotically before dashing after the women, who fled laughing. When she finally caught a woman, she simulated sexual intercourse with her while the audience looked on gleefully.[100] Temples to Legba appeared all over Dahomey in the shape of tiny thatched huts only about three feet high with four posts and no walls. Inside sat a wooden carving of Legba displaying an enormous erect penis. Inexplicably, a few Legba carvings were female, with enormous breasts. Dahomeans regularly left offerings of food for Legba, and when these were eaten by dogs, people were not displeased, because dogs were sacred to Legba and were greatly loved and always well treated by the Dahomeans, probably more so than by any other West African people.[101] Legba was a trickster who brought an element of unpredictability into life. He (she) had the power to protect people or to make their lives perilous. But Legba also possessed tricks to help people evade the rigid rules of government. Legba was venerated by all cult groups and in every home. All the Fon people of Dahomey sought to propitiate him.[102]

The world of Dahomey was so filled with supernatural forces that it was sometimes impossible to separate natural phenomena from supernatural ones. In addition to their pantheons of gods, the terrestrial spirits of the dead—some friendly, some decidedly not—lurked in trees, rivers, and marshes. There were witches, too, and sorcerers of all sorts. Divination was in constant demand to determine what people needed to do to escape harm, who was responsible for it, and what might happen next. Kings were as dependent on diviners as the most fearful commoner.[103] Dahomeans could become possessed by supernatural beings, too. Many of these supernatural beings and forces helped people to cope with the problems of life, whereas others created problems. Still others were simply part of the world, unseen, unknowable, unchangeable. Religion and everyday life were inseparable.

As in many places, people in the countryside looked upon city-dwellers with fear and suspicion, and city people felt themselves greatly superior, but for the most part, the people of Dahomey were content with their lives. And while Dahomey may have been better controlled by its government than many societies, less tolerant of crime, and somewhat more respectful of women, from what we have seen thus far, it was, in many respects, not greatly different from many other West African societies. But Dahomey's vitality and very survival depended on people's perceived majesty of the king and his ability to inspire devotion, obedience, and awe. In the next chapter, we examine how he did so with such extraordinary success.

3

The Creation of Majesty

To create and maintain such profound respect that one's people would be unquestioningly loyal and obedient was a daunting challenge for any monarch, whether tsar, sultan, or West African king, and most monarchs—and not a few dictators—around the world went to great lengths to demonstrate their greatness through military parades, lavish displays of wealth, and ceremonial affirmation of their majesty. It is not known exactly how Dahomey's first king began this task in the early 1600s, but there were many models of semidivine kingship from neighboring states to choose from. Dahomey's leaders were remarkably successful in borrowing various aspects of these models to establish a world that not only separated their monarch from other Dahomeans but also elevated him above everyone else without declaring him to be divine. To bring about this near apotheosis, the court created bards and singers to recite their monarchs' virtues and praise their accomplishments to the common people. Monarchs also dressed sumptuously, were catered to by hordes of attendants, and were honored by such deferential rules of etiquette that there could be no doubt about their absolute majesty. And not least important, they were guarded everywhere they went by armed and uniformed women guards, who often displayed their might and their loyalty in parades, dances, and military exercises.

Even European visitors were impressed by Dahomean kings' ostentatious displays of wealth, especially when valuables were exhibited in regal parades and given away in dramatic ceremonies. When Dahomey's large professional armies of both men and women paraded, their numbers, flamboyance, and military menace dramatically reaffirmed the king's authority. And each year, during a great ceremony when the king ordered that some 100 criminals and war prisoners be decapitated in public, he again demonstrated his power. Neighboring kings in West Africa, like others in more distant parts of the world, used similar devices to establish their power, but few anywhere did so with as much success as the kings of Dahomey. One historian who looked back on Dahomey concluded, "The Abomey kingdom in the nineteenth century constituted an almost perfect example of absolute monarchy."[1] As we have seen, the monarchy was far from being absolute but that impression was created and maintained with enormous realism.

Royal palaces helped to symbolize the king's separateness and his greatness. No one could enter any of his palaces without his invitation, and except for eunuchs, no man did so after sunset. His principal palace of Simboji in Abomey was an immense congregation of both round and rectangular buildings with thatched roofs. Many buildings had bas-reliefs set into their walls; painted in brilliant colors, they are even today considered works of art, still visited by tourists. The palace's thick mud wall was over twenty feet in height, enclosing several thousand royal wives, many women soldiers, and some hundreds of eunuchs—as many as 8,000 people in all.[2] John Atkins, a British surgeon who visited Abomey early in the eighteenth century, was often favorably impressed by the kingdom, but he described Simboji Palace as "a dirty, large, bamboo building, of a mile or two in circumference; where he (the king) kept a thousand concubines, and divided his time between eating and lust."[3]

Simboji Palace was far more than this; it was a city within a city and the "pivot of political life" for Dahomey, as one observer put it.[4] The king's elegant four-mile-square palace at Cana housed additional wives who lived there permanently, and thousands of his other wives and Amazons would accompany him when he moved from Abomey to Cana, as he did quite often. In addition to these two palaces there were five smaller ones that the king and his palace entourage sometimes visited. The king typically held court outside one of his palace gates, usually reclining on an umbrella-shaded mat while members of his court and various male officials, often joined by their female counterparts, squatted around him. Other women fanned him, and shaded him with umbrellas, while armed women guards looked on vigilantly. All members of his en-tourage were dressed far more grandly than the common people whose complaints and offenses were being deliberated upon, but none as grandly as the king, who wore elegant robes thrown over his shoulders, fine jewelry, and various kinds of headgear. Seemingly every Dahomean man smoked a pipe, but none did so as incessantly, or grandly, as the king, who was always followed by a woman with more tobacco for his silver-plated pipe, another with various means to relight it, and yet another with a gold-plated spittoon.[5]

Mirroring a practice witnessed by Ibn Battuta in 1353 during his visit to the Kingdom of Mali, and one still widespread in West Africa, all Dahomeans, no matter their rank or royal ancestry, had to prostrate themselves upon approaching the presence of the king. Even his highest-ranking ministers and soldiers under arms did so in the same abject manner. Visiting Europeans were permitted merely to bow, but when in the king's presence, all of his Dahomean subjects threw themselves face down on the dusty or muddy ground (depending on the season), then, while still prostrate, threw red dust or mud all over their heads and kissed the ground. Duncan noted that when the prostrated figures finally arose, these previ-ously scrupulously clean and well-dressed people were filthy. He was disgusted by "such absurd, abject humiliation."[6]

A Portuguese visitor interpreted this prostration as an expres-sion of fear:

The inhabitants have such a servile fear of the king, that, when his hammock or palanquin appears, they prostrate themselves to the ground, and, until he has passed, continue throwing earth on their heads in token of submission. Even the officer whom we should denominate the secretary-of-state, and the nobility, are not exempt from this feeling of entire subservience to the will of their sovereign— which they manifest with as much humility as any of their inferior fellow-subjects.[7]

Witnessing these expressions of abject submission by persons of wealth and power must have had a profound effect on the common people, as it was no doubt intended to do. Common people could not know that these expressions were part of a ritual, not true expressions of fear or subservience.

Rituals of subservience were witnessed by Snelgrave as early as the 1720s. After prostrating themselves obsequiously, no Dahomean man or woman could appear before the king wearing a hat, with shoulders uncovered, wearing sandals, or smoking a pipe. All had to sit on the ground rather than a stool. The awe in which the king was held by his subjects was seen in everything that transpired around his presence. Even a symbol of the monarch such as a royal scepter or emblem carried by a messenger evoked awe and subservience. Covered with cloth until the messenger reached the designated recipient, the symbol of royalty was uncovered before the message was delivered; then all present prostrated themselves as if the king himself were present.[8]

The king also enhanced his majestic mystique by the practice of never being seen to eat or drink in public, leading many Dahomeans to believe that he did not need to eat at all, or to sleep, and might therefore be truly godlike.[9] He also extended some of his awe-inspiring powers to his wives. Whenever royal wives left the palace, always preceded by some female slaves ringing a small bell, all women had to turn their backs, and all men, including European visitors, had to move some distance away from their path before turning their backs, a custom that greatly annoyed the Europeans! Duncan referred to it as "one of the most intolerable nuisances."[10]

Although often outspoken behind the scenes, the king's highest officials were bound to absolute obedience in public and were often severely punished for any public sign of disrespect, not to mention any breaches of the monarch's orders or wishes. Some were even executed. The king also attempted to maintain, although never with more than limited success, the appearance of control over the priesthoods that directed Dahomey's religious cults, many of which were led by women. However, thanks to his elaborate intelligence-gathering system, the king was able to control not only the distribution of property in his domain but the activities of the lineages as well. In all this, he was aided greatly by his many wives and the women "doubles," who kept him reliably informed about almost everything, as well as by his court, which consistently supported the ceremonies and rules of etiquette that created both reverence and fear in the minds of his people. Europeans marveled that the prime minister and his female double complied with such a seemingly degrading practice as prostration before the king. One wrote, "It is extraordinary that while the *miegan* and the *mayo* wallow in the mud in royal presence, they have, if united, actually more power than their royal master."[11]

The first European to spend any unguarded moments with a Dahomean king was a British trader with the unforgettable name of Bullfinch Lamb (sometimes written "Lambe"). Lamb was in Ardra when Dahomean troops took the town in 1724, capturing him in the process. Taken to the Dahomean commander with great courtesy, he was offered a dram of brandy before being carried to Abomey in a hammock. These courtesies to a "white man" were in stark contrast to the savagery of the fighting. Lamb said that after the battle headless bodies lay everywhere, and "had it rain'd blood, it could not have lain thicker on the ground."[12] Once Lamb arrived in Abomey, King Agaja treated his white captive as an honored guest, providing him with two well-appointed houses, numerous servants, and many "wives," as Lamb called them, women who were actually royal prostitutes. Often, when the king was carried some distance in his grand hammock, Lamb accompanied him on a horse Agaja had provided him. In public, Agaja frequently displayed what Lamb described as immense amounts of gold and other wealth, receiving every obeisance from his people. But when he was alone with Lamb, he dropped most of his affectations of grandeur to display his love of toys—he badly wanted a kite after Lamb described one. He often chatted informally with Lamb, and he also carried a Latin mass book, studying it as if he could read, then scribbling gibberish on a piece of paper.[13] Lamb continually pleaded with Agaja to be released, only to be told, politely to be sure, that, in effect, he was a white trophy whose presence in Abomey raised Agaja's stature.

Lamb wrote letters appealing to his countrymen to ransom him, suggesting that sending a "cast-off" white or mulatto "whore" to Abomey would win Agaja's heart, and in the same letter paradoxically praising the beauty and elegance of Agaja's many wives, who he said numbered 2,000:

> And when one Hundred and Sixty, or two Hundred of them goes [sic] with Little Pots for Water, they one Day wear rich silk Waist-cloathes, called Arse-clouts; another Day they all wear Scarlet Cloaths with three or four large Strings of Coral about their Necks, and their Headers sometimes in Crimson, sometimes in Green, and sometimes Blue Velvet Cloaths with Silver-gilt Staffs in their Hands like Golden Canes.[14]

After almost two years, Lamb was finally released with a promise on his honor to return, a pledge he did not keep.

But palace life in Dahomey was not all toys and beautifully dressed women. Soon after Lamb's capture, Agaja ordered an attack on Whydah, and although the king of Whydah—"the largest and fattest man I ever saw," Lamb wrote—escaped in a hammock, his kingdom fell easily, and many prisoners were taken. According to Lamb, the Dahomean commander ordered "all the boys in camp . . . Some of whom were not above Seven or Eight Years of Age, to cut off the heads of all the Aged and Wounded among the Captives that were unmerchantable."[15] Because the boys were so small, the butchery was agonizingly slow, but as a display of Agaja's wrath it was no doubt terrible to see and must have left a lasting impression.

The return of a victorious army was another opportunity to honor the king. In 1727, Captain William Snelgrave of the British Royal Navy was invited to watch the return of King Agaja's victorious full-time male troops, followed by thousands of baggage carriers and boys who carried the soldiers' shields while learning as much as they could about the craft of war. As noted earlier, as the troops "passed the King's Gate, every Soldier prostrated himself, and kissed the Ground; then rose with such agility, as was very surprising."[16] While a throng of spectators looked on, they drilled, fired salutes to the king, and displayed their martial ardor for all to witness. Snelgrave wrote that "this sight was well worth seeing even by us Europeans."[17]

In addition to conquests that enhanced their power and the return of victorious troops, Dahomey's kings regularly staged dramatic festivities to showcase their power. During the 1770s, British slave trader Robert Norris was invited to join King Kpengla to witness a parade that would take place before a huge gathering of common people in Abomey. After bowing to the king, Norris was directed to a chair, where four slaves held a large umbrella over him to protect him from the sun while he and other members of the king's court were treated to a vast meal. Because Dahomean kings maintained cooks trained by European traders at the coast, a European visitor would be provided with dishes from his homeland, usually served on fine china.[18] As all in the court except the king gorged themselves, a band featuring trumpets, flutes, bells, and drums played loudly while a huge crowd danced delightedly. When one band tired, it was replaced. In all, four bands alternated. When the feasting ended, the king walked to the head of the parade, followed by twenty-four armed and magnificently uniformed Amazons. The king danced "for some time, to convince his subjects of his health and activity, to their inexpressible joy and satisfaction; which they manifested in the loudest acclamations."[19] The king then distributed large numbers of cowries to the musicians.

The festivities were renewed the following day, when Norris was conducted toward the palace.

On each side of the entrance, were three human heads that had been cut off the night before; and in the center was erected a lofty tent, shaped like a sugar loaf, about fifty feet high and forty feet wide; it was open below, and rested on a circular range of small iron rails, through which the king could have a view of what passed in the parade. He soon made his appearance, and seated himself (amidst the shouts and acclamations of the people) under his tent, on an elegant armed chair, covered with crimson velvet, and ornamented with carving and gilding. I was placed under the shade of a large umbrella, the *Mallays* [Arab traders] on my right, and about thirty eunuchs, with each a bright iron rod in their hands, and dressed like women, on my left hand: after the music had played about half an hour, with the confused noise of which, and the shouts and songs of multitude, I was almost stunned; a droll Harlequin entertained the king with an odd sort of dance, and fired occasionally a blunderbuss with five barrels, which gave the king so much satisfaction, that he sent him five *cabefs* (40 each) of *cowries*.[20]

The procession was led by over 100 men, carrying blunderbusses, marching two abreast. They were followed by 15 of the king's daughters, attended by some 50 female slaves. Next marched over 730 of the king's wives, carrying all manner of provisions and liquors for the feast that would follow. The wives were followed by a troop of 90 uniformed women under arms, marching to the beat of a drum. While Norris ate breakfast, the parade continued with six troops of 70 heavily armed Amazons in each. The woman who led the procession was so "sacred" that she was hidden from sight by an umbrella and long strips of leather and taffeta. More women warriors and wives followed, entertaining the king with their songs and dances as they passed by. His favorites entered his tent to pay their respects, receiving valuable gifts of cowries in return. These women were followed by bands of the king's younger children. More troops followed, each one led by two large British flags. These women entertained the king with their songs and dances:

Four of them particularly engaged my attention: their dress was too extravagant to be described; and each had a long tail fixed to her rump, which seemed to be a slip of leopard's skin, sewed up and stuffed; which, by a dexterous wriggle of their hips they whirled round with surprising velocity, like a sling. These likewise had a share of their master's bounty, and marched off loaden [sic] with cowries.[21]

The eunuchs, dressed as women, then sang the king's praises, listing his titles, and proclaiming his greatness in the most extravagant terms. Then came more women, whose dresses and ornaments were even more grand with gaudy silks, silver bracelets, and coral necklaces and beads. Following a band of forty women wearing silver helmets came an assortment of the king's furniture and trinkets, including fine swords, silver-mounted guns, muskets, hundreds of gold- or silver-headed canes, and many other articles, which were all held up for the admiring crowd to see. That evening after dinner, a female dwarf danced for the king, performing very well: "She seemed to be about thirty years old, and measured only two feet seven inches high, was without any deformity, and tolerably well shaped."[22]

Three-quarters of a century later, Burton described a similarly grand parade led by soldiers in brass helmets with huge dangling black horsetails. The king rode behind the troops under four white umbrellas while three parasols—yellow, purple, and reddish blue—were waved over him as fans. Next came a band whose many rattles, cymbals, and drums added to the excitement and the noise. Slaves followed, loaded with food and drink. Sometimes riding in a cab, sometimes in a chair, and once, carried aloft, the king made six circuits of the square, amounting to fully five miles of dust and pandemonium. Burton noticed that the king looked weary and cross, "an expression not unfrequent upon the brow of royalty in all lands."[23]

Burton continued, describing how the king and his most elegant canopies were taken to the massed Amazons, who, led by skirmishers firing their weapons and ringing sharp bells, sprinted into the square, dancing and firing muskets and blunderbusses before retiring. The royal bodyguard next appeared, led by young women who performed with great agility. Following a parade of women with twelve "fancy flags" and male soldiers with crimson leather shields, the king was carried in a hammock of yellow silk by a dozen women until a "heavy salute of blunderbusses" was fired and the procession finally ended at 5:45 P.M. "with the usual finale to a Dahoman parade—a headache."[24]

And so it was with every public demonstration of the king's wealth and power. Although the wealth that allowed at least forty Amazons to wear fine silver helmets when Norris watched them parade was much depleted by the time of Burton's visit in 1863, parades still involved thousands of participants and many more onlookers. Before the king and other high officials finally arrived in grand carriages, including one made to resemble an elephant, all manner of colorful silk umbrellas and flags from many nations had passed by, thousands of muskets had been fired into the air, heavily armed Amazons had danced athletically and sung their songs of utter devotion and fearlessness, and dozens of bands had played very loudly but, to European ears, tunelessly. All of this created immense enthusiasm among the parade watchers, who screamed their approval.

European visitors to Cana and Abomey often heard Amazons singing within the palaces, apparently practicing for their performances during the military parades in which they played such a prominent role. The military bands, composed of drums, horns, rattles, tambourines, whistles, flutes, and iron gongs, were little less than deafening. One European observer after another complained about the earsplitting racket, often referring to it in the most negative terms imaginable.[25] While the bands played, the Amazons did not attempt to sing over the din; instead they danced, sometimes solo, sometimes in groups. Some European observers, like Italian priest Father Borghero, were critical of what they saw, characterizing their dancing as "contortions, stompings, caperings of all kinds."[26] Burton wrote that "nothing could be less graceful or more deficient in the poetry of motion."[27] A few years later, Skertchly compared their movements to those of "St. Vitus' Dance" but admitted that the women's frenzied displays of energy were nonetheless "impressive."[28]

But other observers who were there during the same period were captivated by the Amazons' dancing. A French naval officer wrote in 1861, "We couldn't believe we were in Dahomey; even long study could not produce dancers more graceful or nimble."[29] Two years later another Frenchman, this one a naval surgeon, wrote that he was "surprised and enchanted," saying that "many times I had seen the dances and heard the songs of various negro tribes . . . , but I had never encountered anything comparable, even remotely, to what we were seeing."[30] Despite this diversity of opinion by Europeans about the Amazons' dancing, all who wrote about the reaction of the Dahomean crowd that watched concluded that they were enraptured by what they saw—Amazons displaying a near frenzy of martial fervor in gymnastic dancing featuring their swords and muskets that sometimes lasted for three hours. They were vivid evidence of the king's might.

The crowd also listened intently when the Amazons sang. Sometimes as soloists, sometimes in harmony, they sang with tremendous energy, extolling the virtues of the king, their own loyalty to him, and their commitment to destroying Dahomey's enemies. Their songs were well rehearsed, as even Burton admitted, referring to the Amazons as "indefatigable singers," and other Europeans were impressed by their well-practiced voices.[31] Burton noted that although these many songs by Amazons were meant to impress the court and the crowds of commoners alike as brilliant improvisations, the songs were the product of repeated rehearsals, as anyone passing by the palace could easily hear.

The dancing and singing were undeniably dramatic, but these parades also featured many hundreds of men, women, and even children who slowly walked by, simply displaying objects of beauty or wealth. There were large numbers of cowrie shells, often tied together into a round ball called a *head*. All manner of cloth was displayed, as was food, from baskets of fruit to calabashes of beer and even bottles of European liquor. Beads, armlets, and bracelets adorned everyone who paraded by, displaying polished human skulls, drums, umbrellas, a rocking horse, rattles, chains, foot stools, wood carvings, metal soup tureens, urns, red earthenware filled with unknown substances, books, statuettes, porcelain jars, a Chinese vase, a European clock, an old cut-glass chandelier, plates of china, drinking glasses, brass shields, and everywhere there was dazzlingly bright clothing of every color. When a full day of such promenading ended, the crowd must have been exhausted. Certainly, the European onlookers were.

Festive parades like those witnessed by Norris and Burton a century apart took place on various occasions throughout the year—the departure of an army for a campaign, the army's victorious return, a visit by a European dignitary. But none could match the drama, extravagance, and grandeur of the events that occurred each year during the dry season. Known to Europeans as the "customs" as we have seen, these annual ceremonies involved great festivities, the exchange of wealth between the people of Dahomey and the king, and the public execution of criminals and war prisoners—the former to dramatize law and order, the latter as a means of thanking the deities for success in war and ensuring future well-being. Most Europeans who were present during these week-long activities deplored the human sacrifice that they saw—and the cannibalism that they believed took place out of their sight—but they could not deny the power of these annual "customs" in the creation of awe and fear around the person of Dahomey's king. Most Europeans were seemingly unaware that these dramatic events were followed by two or more weeks of vital behind-the-scenes legislative activity by some 300 delegates to Dahomey's Great Council, as their legislature was known.

The "customs" began with the construction of a building to house those about to be decapitated. Resembling a village church, with a barnlike room and a tower, it held twenty or so intended victims. They sat on stools, their arms tied to posts in front of them and their necks also secured to these large, firmly planted posts. All were dressed as state criminals with long white nightcaps, calico shirts with a crimson patch on the left breast, and a loincloth. Their treatment at this stage of the "customs" was anything but barbaric. Each captive had a guard seated behind him to fan away the flies, and each prisoner received no fewer than four good meals a day. At night, they were allowed to lie down to sleep but were closely watched. Because it was traditional that some would receive the king's pardon—an excellent device for preventing attempted escapes—when Burton saw such men in 1863, they were chattering happily with one another and marking time to the music they could hear outside.[32]

A similar nonchalance on the part of the condemned men was reported by other European visitors. Almost a century earlier, when Robert Norris witnessed the annual "customs," he, too, saw men tied to posts awaiting execution, and he also noticed that they were beating time to the music of the parading bands. Despite the prisoners' nonchalance, Norris wrote that thirty-six men and thirty-two horses had already been beheaded, their bodies left in the sun to rot. The stench overwhelmed him. He was also shocked to see two naked men who had been clubbed to death hanging from twenty-foot-tall posts at the entrance to the marketplace where the executions took place. Their genitals had been cut off, and vultures were tearing out their intestines and devouring them as Norris hurried away in horror.[33] As a subsequent king once explained to another European, this scene was meant to evoke similar emotions in ordinary Dahomeans.

Most free Dahomean adults excepting the very old and infirm were expected to attend the ceremony that began on the first day, when a high official took all horses from their wealthy owners, holding them until the end of the customs, when they could be redeemed in return for cowrie shells. As a warning shot was fired inside the palace, a brightly uniformed corps of Amazons led the king under a colorful umbrella through the dense crowd toward an elevated, thatched platform that overlooked the square. Nearby, the crowd could see another nineteen potential victims tied to posts awaiting their fate while an enormous throng danced around them, singing and expressing wild merriment. After snapping fingers with Burton (the Dahomean equivalent of a handshake), King Glele returned to his royal viewing stand, where he was surrounded by more Amazons in full parade uniforms, their "gun barrels bristling upwards," as Burton put it.[34] Amply provided with an array of food, many members of his royal entourage gathered behind the king as they made ready to watch the opening-day festivities.

Many thousands of people, including hundreds of small children, watched male and female soldiers dance and fire their weapons until King Glele made his appearance. A tall man who towered over his wives, Glele was light-skinned and richly dressed, his hands clasped behind his back. There were murmurs of applause, and his subjects beamed with admiration. He was followed by sundry wives, each with a different and usually elaborate hairdo, including one with two tufts like large upright bears' ears and another with hair resembling a six-inch-tall fez. Some women had completely shaved heads, and others had shaved all but a small tuft or two of hair. After a cymbal clang brought the crowd to silence, the king made a speech honoring his ancestors, and promising to maintain the glorious ceremony about to begin in the future as it had been maintained in the past. He briefly pounded on two large drums before retiring behind a curtain held by his wives and drinking something, perhaps the gin he had thanked Burton for giving him a few minutes earlier. After a short pause, he returned and sang "to the great delight of his listeners,"[35] then danced with movements that Burton described as "comparatively kingly and dignified."[36] Jesters then capered about and, pointing to the king, shouted that he was "'sweet, sweet, sweet as a white man,'" a declaration that Burton did not attempt to explain. While Amazons danced acrobatically, the king walked to the male spectators, and using his forefinger to wipe sweat from his brow, flicked his sweat over them, to their obvious delight, an act Burton also did not explain.

After being fanned by some of his wives, Glele danced six separate times as if he were pantomiming the beheading of captives. He then sang with his staff uplifted, apparently in homage to his father, before personally distributing yellow bead necklaces and rolls of blue and pink cotton to various dignitaries. Next, scores of women appeared from the palace displaying all manner of valuables while new wives recently taken by the king crouched humbly. That procession was followed by a series of speeches flattering his greatness in excessive, and sometimes patently ridiculous, exaggerations. Following this long effusion of praise, a number of government officials and army officers were promoted, amid much fanfare and exhortations to them by the king to be brave and loyal. All of this was witnessed by the captives scheduled to die.

Because of the searingly dry winds of the Harmattan, the king postponed the second day's festivities from December 29 to December 30, 1863. The next morning began with eunuchs and hunchbacks leading a large band of Amazons followed by more women, who good-naturedly teased the Europeans as they passed by. Then came dignitaries on horseback as the dust and heat rose to torment the foreign observers. Despite the soaring heat, an all-male band paraded back and forth clanging cymbals, followed by a female band, while groups of singers promenaded and the square was filled with frenetic dancers.

This frenzy continued until late afternoon, when the king finally appeared, circling the square three times to great applause before taking his seat in the pavilion, where more of his wealth—this time 1,000 yards of fine European cloth—was displayed to deafening cheers. After sitting on his divan for some time while several of his wives fanned him, the king suddenly arose, stripped to his satin, yellow-flowered shorts, and began to dance energetically while swinging a billhook as if decapitating victims. Shouts of joy, exclamations of wonder, and discharges of muskets and cannon punctuated his performance, which included pointing a musket at the crowd and pretending to fire while they burst into laughter. After openly drinking some rum from a brass cup attached to the polished skull of a conquered king (an apparent exception to his usual rule of public abstinence), Glele danced with his silver sword between his teeth while tossing the skull from one hand to the other.

The third day began much as the second had, with dancing, singing, and women priests parading by as horns and rattles created a tremendous din. Soon, however, the king walked to the front of his pavilion and began to throw strings of cowries into the crowd, who fought over them until blood flowed. When the uproar ended, parties of hunchbacks and dwarfs danced with great enthusiasm until the king walked over to the shed where the bound victims sat and then threw strings of cowries toward them, which their attendants placed on their heads. At that point, Richard Burton was given to understand that some might be pardoned if he interceded on their behalf. Telling the king that mercy was the prerogative of kings, Burton did so, and "nearly half" were untied and placed on all fours to hear the royal clemency. Burton did not record what became of them after their pardons.

The fourth day began on January 1, 1864, with more athletic dancing by groups of women, particularly Amazons, who loudly promised to conquer the Egba city of Abeokuta. The king made several speeches to the effect that only the destruction of the "insolent" enemy city of Abeokuta could restore his honor. There followed a long series of processions by various kinds of women, from small girls to beautiful princesses and aged grandmothers, carrying valuables to be given to distinguished Dahomeans later that night. While these processions passed by, a bamboo railing was being emplaced along the road from the palace to a large marketplace, where the executions were scheduled for that evening. It was usual for the killing to take place on two consecutive nights, but this apparently varied. It was also customary for women to be killed by Amazons inside the palace while male executioners killed the male victims in front of the king and the public, but this practice, too, was known to vary.

The first European to write about executions on the coast of Benin was the Dutch slaver William Bosman in 1698, when he saw slaves sacrificed in what was the still-independent Kingdom of Whydah. He saw eleven killed: "What with Hacking, Piercing, Tormenting, etc., they endure a Thousand Deaths."[37] One victim was decapitated by a six-year-old, who took fully an hour to complete his mission because he lacked sufficient strength for the act. Executions in Dahomey were conducted with far greater ceremony than those at Whydah, as we learn from Snelgrave, who witnessed them in 1727. Snelgrave and his companions were led through a huge crowd to one of four small stages raised about five feet off the ground. The first victim Snelgrave saw

> was a comely old man, between fifty and sixty years of age. His hands were tied behind him; and in his behaviour, he showed a brave and undaunted mind, nothing like fear appearing in him. As he stood upright by the stage, a *Feticheer*, or priest, laid his hand on his head saying some words of consecration, which lasted about two minutes. Then he gave the sign of execution to a man that stood behind the victim with a broad sword, who immediately struck him on the nape of the neck, with such force, that the head was severed at one blow, from the body; whereupon the rabble gave a great shout. The head was cast on the stage, and the body, after having lain a little while on the ground, that the blood might drain from it, was carried away by slaves and thrown in a place adjoining the camp.[38]

Snelgrave went on to say that the men to be executed approached the stage "bold and unconcerned," but that the "cries of the poor women and children were very moving."[39] These women victims were killed in the palace without a male audience. If children were executed, no subsequent European visitor mentioned it.

Snelgrave later asked a Dahomean army officer why so many prisoners who could profitably have been sold were sacrificed. He was told that this sacrifice was necessary to appease the gods and ensure future success in war. When Snelgrave asked why so many older men were sacrificed, he was told that the king personally chose the victims from the war prisoners taken to Abomey and because these older men had been chiefs in their own country they would plot against their masters and cause disruption. He added that because of their age no European would buy them in any event.[40] The next day Snelgrave and his party, which included a Dutch slave trader, passed by two piles of some 400 bodies in all.

Snelgrave was told that the common people had "feasted" on these bodies as "holy food."[41] Over a century later, John Duncan, a former British army officer, witnessed more executions, describing them as "clumsy." He was appalled by the sight of an old man who stood by with a calabash to catch the blood and drink it. When the man added some rum to the blood and offered the calabash to Duncan, the Englishman refused it in disgust.[42]

In early 1864, when Burton visited the palace the morning after similar executions had taken place, he saw six corpses dressed in their white criminal shirts, seated on stools on a scaffold some forty feet high, and farther on, he saw three naked bodies hanging by their heels from a tall post. These men had been emasculated, but all retained their heads. In all, he saw twenty-three bodies, most of them decapitated. Later that day, seemingly all of Abomey paraded past the royal grandstand. Wearing every costume imaginable, heavily armed men and women passed by, most of them puffing on their pipes. A few men wore black frock coats with coral necklaces; then came the great male officials of Dahomey followed by their female counterparts, some of whom had human skulls or jaws hanging from their waists. The viceroy from Whydah wore a tall chimney-pot hat, and others wore everything from European straw hats to sailors' caps and Dahomean white skullcaps with blue crocodiles on the sides. When all had finally assembled, they kissed the ground four times in unison, clapped their hands three times, and then rose and presented arms. After some chants and a song about the planned destruction of Abeokuta, slave girls brought calabashes brimming with food and others containing much rum. Before leaving the scene of celebration, each group— archers, poets, dwarfs, priests, soldiers, hunchbacks, officials, singers, dancers, and, loudest of all, Amazons—sang the king's praises, describing his greatness in songs punctuated by sharp exclamations. As they did so, dozens of the king's carriages, some made in America, paraded past, pulled by slaves rather than horses.

Next came various other women in red nightcaps with a silver shark on each side; then came bands of small girls with various flags, older women in fools' caps of blue and red, a man with a huge scimitar, and another with a British flag—all kinds of bands and singers.[43] Only after seven grueling hours of parading had passed did the crowd begin to disperse.

Sir Richard Burton was the first foreigner to discover that the king's "double" as "king of the countryside," or "bush king," conducted his own, less grand "customs."[44] Presiding in a rude palace six miles from Abomey, which Burton was not allowed to enter, Addo-kpon, as he was known, greeted Burton and his entourage with the bodies of mutilated men hanging outside the city gate. After introductory ceremonies a good deal less grand than those at Abomey, the so-called bush king asked Burton to dance with him before the large crowd, which Burton did, to the delight of those who watched. The next morning, more corpses were found sitting or hanging outside the palace walls, apparently sixteen in all, a relatively large number for a small "custom" like this one.

On the fifth day of the custom, Burton arrived in front of Addo-kpon's palace at 5 A.M., whereupon hundreds of soldiers erupted from it with bands playing and muskets firing before Burton once again danced with the bush king. More singing, dancing, and drumming followed until King Glele arrived to join the ceremony. He was honored by the usual parade of soldiers, bands, and singers, as well as rousing martial displays by excited Amazons, before he danced for the jubilant crowd holding Burton gently by the wrist. There followed another enormous parade of subjects passing in review.

On the final day of this annual ceremony, an immense crowd of people gathered before a stage in Abomey, where the king, various Dahomean dignitaries, and European visitors threw all manner of valuables, such as cloth, coral beads, and cowries, into the crowd and people scrambled and fought for their possession. What Robert Norris had witnessed almost a century earlier was repeated in 1864. First, the king threw cowries into the crowd; then, his *ahosi* flung the remainder of the goods indiscriminately among the multitude. Some of the white men also did so. Finally, a man tied "neck and heels," a muzzled alligator, and several pigeons with their wings clipped were thrown from the stage into the crowd, where people scrambled to cut off the heads of the man and the animals, "to the great amusement of the King."[45] Those lucky enough to carry off the heads of the victims received a valuable present. British naval-surgeon-turned-slave-trader Archibald Dalzel reported, "This is the last human sacrifice at the Customs, and is a part of the ceremony which the Whites seldom stay to see performed; but, if report may be credited, the carcass of the human victim is almost wholly devoured, as all the mob below will have a taste of it."[46]

On another occasion of the customs in 1772, the king sent his half-heads to invite various European governors at the coast to come to Abomey to witness it. A British witness wrote that he found King Kpengla seated among 400 of his wives, all elegantly dressed. Nearby, six women were on their knees, with profoundly pained expressions on their faces. Kpengla called for a bundle, which he untied to reveal five swords. He gave these to five of his older, decidedly hefty wives. While the six women captives knelt before him, he declared:

> "These women were brought from Apee by my army; I took them home, domesticated them in my family—treated them as my wives;—but, not contented, they made their escape to their native country; where, however, they found nothing but the ground and the trees; for every thing else had been destroyed by my troops. They afterwards surrendered themselves to the King of Ardrah; but he was too just to keep them, and has therefore sent them back to me, to receive the proper reward for their ingratitude."[47]

One woman who had a suckling child was told that she would be spared for the time being, but that soon she would suffer the same fate as the others. The five other women were ordered to kneel, with their faces touching the ground, while the king's women began to decapitate them so clumsily that the onlooking Europeans were shocked. One woman had her head severed from her body after "only" four strokes, but it took fully twenty minutes for the others to die, as the king stood over them, instructing his wives: "'Not that way—hold your cutlass thus—give it me—'tis so—imagine you are chopping wood.' Thus did the hellish monster direct the ministers of his cruelty to cut off heads, with as much apathy as if indeed he had been chopping wood."[48]

Soon after, King Kpengla explained to the slave trader Dalzel why he carried out the annual ceremony called customs: "You have seen me kill many men at the Customs. . . . Some heads I order to be placed at my door; others to be strewed about the market-place, that people may stumble upon them when they little expect such a sight. This gives a grandeur to my Customs, far beyond the display of fine things which I buy. This makes my enemies fear me, and gives me such a name in the bush."[49]

Kpengla added that if he neglected this "indispensable duty," his ancestors would not "suffer" him to live:

> "Would they not trouble me day and night, and say, that I sent nobody to serve them; that I was only solicitous about my own name, and forgetful of my ancestors? White men are not acquainted with these circumstances; but I now tell you, that you may hear, and know, and inform your countrymen, why Customs are made, and will be made, as long as black men continue to possess their own country."[50]

Three-quarters of a century later, King Gezo told another visitor why the customs and the slave trade could not be abolished:

> The ceremonies and customs to be observed annually, which had been handed down to him from his forefathers entailed upon him a vast outlay of money. These could not be abolished. The form of his government could not be suddenly changed, without causing such a revolution as would deprive him of his throne, and precipitate his kingdom into a state of anarchy.[51]

Two years later, Forbes added this about the authority of King Gezo (1850):

There is something fearful in the state of subjection in which, in outward show, the kings of Dahomey hold their highest officers; yet, when the system is examined, these prostrations are merely keeping up the ancient custom. And although no man's head in Dahomey can be considered warranted for twenty-four (hours), still the great chief himself would find his tottering if one of these customs was omitted. There is an iron tyranny which governs all, and over which none appears to have control. . . . Gezu, we are assured has no delight in human sacrifices, and continues these awful scenes solely out of deference to ancient national customs.[52]

To everyone's surprise, especially that of the British, whom Gezo informed of his plans in writing in 1853, Gezo abolished the human sacrifice of war captives, henceforth beheading only criminals. When he died in 1858 of an infection caused when an enemy warrior shot him during a war campaign, it was widely thought by Dahomeans that his death was divine punishment for his sacrilege. His successor, Glele, immediately reinstated the previous pattern of human sacrifice.[53] A few years later, King Glele told priest Peter Bernasko, "If I do not carry them on as usual I am afraid that I should be dethroned or hurt by the subjects."[54]

In that same year, King Glele added this to Commodore Eardley Wilmot about human sacrifice: "'If I were to give up this custom at once, my head would be taken off tomorrow.'"[55] Soon after, Glele gave this explanation to Sir Richard Burton, who had demanded an end to human sacrifice:

"These institutions cannot be stopped in the way you propose. By-and-by, little by little, much may be done—softly, softly, not by threats!"[56]

Burton concluded:

Human sacrifice in Dahome is founded upon a purely religious basis, which not only strengthens but perpetuates the customs. It is a touching instance of the King's filial piety. . . . his subjects would deem it impious were he to curtail or to omit the performance, and suddenly to suppress it would be as if a European monarch were forcibly to abolish prayers for the dead.[57]

A decade later, J. A. Skertchly wrote this:

The "hereafter" of the Dahoman is an eternal continuance of the state being enjoyed by the deceased when on earth. The ghosts are sup- posed to take a great interest in worldly affairs, and to secretly im- press the mind of their protégés with the good advice. . . . This belief is the one great stumbling block against the abolition of the human sacrifices at the Customs. The suppression of these would be looked upon by the popular eye as a direct insult to the protecting spirits of the country, and a general revolt would be the inevitable conse- quence.[58]

As powerful as the annual customs must have been as a means of inspiring awe and fear, the so-called grand customs, held after a king's death, may have been even more so. In addition to a three- day period in which normal daily activity ceased, a king's death could lead to a power scramble as the heir apparent attempted to hold power against his brothers or other princes. After the death of King Kpengla in April 1789, the kingdom fell into chaos, and vio- lence was commonplace, especially among the royal women. Dalzel estimated that 595 women were killed by other royal wives and Amazons, some of them to attend to King Kpengla in the other world.[59] Some of these women apparently willingly took poison to join their husband in the new life, but most appear to have been killed fighting for one side or another in the struggle for succession. Before this particular grand custom was brought to an end three months later, perhaps 1,000 people, including children, had been killed.[60] And in 1860, two eye-witnesses to the grand custom for King Gezo reported that between 700 and 1,000 people were killed.[61]

The felt need to kill so many people at the death of a king and during the annual customs is strong evidence of the strength of Dahomean religious convictions. It is also evidence of aspiring kings' and their supporters' determination to gain power for themselves. They gained this power despite the discontent of a large slave population, the ignorance of easily led common people, and the jealousy and appetite for power of many wealthy, ambitious, and disloyal people. Intrigue dominated palace life, forcing kings to rely ever more on the Amazons for protection and the royal wives as spies. Yet only twice over Dahomey's more than 200-year history did kingly succession lead to open conflict, and these two periods of political disorder were brief. Even following Dahomey's defeat by the French in 1892, when the kingdom was in obvious disarray and King Béhanzin had to go into hiding, social order was maintained and no one among the common people betrayed the fugitive king, even though the French offered a large reward to anyone revealing his whereabouts. Attended by only a handful of people, the king had to remain on the move in remote areas to the north, until he was captured a year later by a French patrol after his brother, the newly installed king, betrayed his whereabouts.[62]

This kind of devotion and social continuity was reinforced by a history of military loyalty, well-crafted social institutions, strong religious beliefs, good government, spies, police, and courts, as well as more subtle unifying factors. Nowhere else in West Africa did kings receive the same degree of loyalty, fear, and awe from the common people that existed in Dahomey. The displays of splendor and power that so often dazzled the people, and the rules of etiquette that required all to humble and even humiliate themselves on all public occasions, played a major role in maintaining that rule.

But so did the presence of a standing army, led by women soldiers who were fiercely loyal to the king. Every other kingdom in West Africa relied on chiefs, wealthy men, and princes to call up militias loyal to them when war beckoned. Dahomean kings also sometimes called for the mobilization of militia when necessary, but they also maintained a professional standing army led by women as its elite troops and its guarantors of royal rule. How these women soldiers triumphed and died in battle is the subject of the next chapter.

This 1851 illustration of an Amazon musketeer is the first serious attempt to depict a woman soldier of Dahomey. Her belt holds a club and dagger. The severed male head is still dripping blood. A military unit lined up in the distance may also represent Amazons. (F. E. Forbes, Dahomey and the Dahomans, 2 vols. (London, 1851), vol. I, opp. p. 23.)

Two romanticized Amazon archers in an 1863 engraving, one holding aloft two freshly cut enemy heads. (A. Répin, "Voyage au Dahomey," Le Tour du Monde, 1863, 2d semester, p. 96.)

Amazon musicians with a gourd rattle, a drum, and a (vague)
trumpet in the background. (A. Bouët, "Le royaume du
Dahomey," L'Illustration, no. 492, July 31, 1852, p. 72.)

Two Amazon officers with long muskets and horns of rank on their heads. (A. Bouët, "Le royaume du Dahomey," L'Illustration, no. 492, July 31, 1852, p. 72.)

Dahomeans at the Zoological Gardens of the Bois de Boulogne, 1891. (Collection Musée de L'Homme, Paris.)

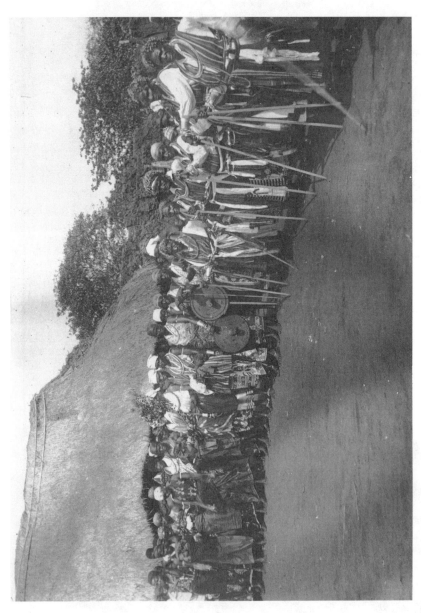

The Amazons (from Luc Garcia/Le royaume du Dahomé: face à la pénétration coloniale (1875–1894), Editions, Karthala, Paris, 1988)

Armed women with the king at their head going to war. (Archibald Dalzel, The History of Dahomey: An Inland Kingdom of Africa, (Frank Cass and Co. Ltd.), London, 1967.)

Public procession of the kings women. (Archibald Dalzel, The History of Dahomey: An Inland Kingdom of Africa, (Frank Cass and Co. Ltd.), London, 1967.)

Detail of a cotton wall hanging with silk and muslin embroideries depicting a campaign of King Glélé against his neighbors, the Nago people. (Collection Musée de L'Homme, Paris.)

4

The Rise and Fall
of the Women Warriors

As the midpoint of the nineteenth century approached, the Amazons were in their ascendancy. They had proven their loyalty to their grateful King Gezo and had come to dominate male officers and soldiers in the army. They had also prospered economically by capturing many war prisoners, receiving money and other payment from the king in return. As one Amazon said in a speech to the Great Council in 1850, "War is our great friend, without it there would be no cloth, nor [jewelry]."[1] This was a strangely "feminine" perspective for women warriors who in their own words had "become men."

From Gezo's successful coup d'état in 1818 until the mid-1840s, the slave trade that the Amazons had done so much to maintain enriched almost everyone in Dahomey. Even though most French and British slave traders had left Dahomey, Brazilian traders aggressively moved in and grew wealthy, as did members of the royal lineage and various high officials. So did many common people who grew food supplies for the slave ships, and some city people also did well as employees of the traders. However, in 1843, Britain imposed a naval blockade that soon limited the trade and threatened to end it altogether.

At the same time, the newly powerful Egba city-state of Abeokuta to the east began to compete openly with Dahomey for the capture and sale of slaves, shipping them not through Whydah but through Porto Novo to the east. When Britain sent diplomats, missionaries, arms, and even military advisers to the fast-growing city of Abeokuta, Dahomean hostility rose to a new extreme, and so did the enmity of the Egba. In 1844, this hostility burst into actual warfare as Egba troops from Abeokuta surprised and defeated a small Dahomean force near the slave port of Porto Novo. Soon after, a weak Dahomean attack on Abeokuta was beaten off. Gezo himself barely avoided capture, thanks to his Amazons, many of whom died defending him. He lost his royal stool and a near-sacred umbrella from which were hung many magical charms.[2] After these embarrassing and economically threatening defeats, talk of war against Abeokuta dominated the Great Council during the annual customs, with royal drummers and singers haranguing the delegates about the need to avenge the defeats of 1844.

Urged on by the Afro-Brazilian slave traders, the king joined with male army officers, and many delegates to the Great Council, in calling for an attack on Abeokuta. Others, among them Dahomeans who could profit from an expanded trade in palm oil much more than they could from slavery, feared that war with the populous Egba people at the large and formidable city of Abeokuta would lead to defeat. The city was enclosed by a wall and held well over 100,000 people, many of the men having muskets; there were a few cannon as well.[3] Many Amazons also had doubts. During the Great Council of 1850, Forbes heard an Amazon officer angrily berate male army officers for the poor performance of male soldiers in a recent battle against a much weaker foe.[4] Arguing that such inadequate male troops could not take Abeokuta, several Amazon officers recommended a policy of directing slave raids against weaker targets to the north.[5] In response, a male officer accused the Amazons of cowardice, infuriating these proud women.

Except for those few Amazons who had become associated with prominent Afro-Brazilian slave traders who favored such an attack because a victory would eliminate the Egba as a slave trade rival, all the Amazons appear to have opposed war with Abeokuta, but at the Great Council of 1850, the women warriors lost their case.[6] After days of bitter controversy, the Amazons capitulated, and all the women soldiers publicly swore their allegiance to King Gezo, promising to destroy Abeokuta.[7] By this time various British visitors, including the Royal Navy commander, F. E. Forbes, who witnessed these events, were referring to these female soldiers as "Amazons."[8] The designation quickly caught on throughout Europe.

Unlike virtually all previous Dahomean wars, this one against Abeokuta would not follow the traditional pattern of careful ritual preparation, detailed planning, long marches, and a surprise attack just before dawn. When a Dahomean army triumphed, it returned with slaves and booty to a grand welcome; when it lost, the army's commander expected to be executed. During King Gezo's reign, his armies won every major battle they fought until the mid-1840s, when they lost to the Egba at Porto Novo. Now, the entire army would attack seeking vengeance. In the autumn of 1850, King Gezo bluntly told British counsel John Beecroft, who was visiting Abomey from Abeokuta, to remove all the Europeans from that "doomed" city because as soon as the dry season arrived, he would attack Abeokuta and raze it to the ground.[9] Not only was Gezo furious because of past defeats at the hands of the Egba, but in recent months, Egba troops had destroyed twenty-five towns along the border of Dahomey and were threatening more attacks to capture still more slaves, some of them Dahomeans.

Forewarned by Beecroft of the Dahomean preparations for war when the dry season—the traditional time for war—arrived, the Egba population of Abeokuta was on alert day and night. There were many false alarms, with women screaming *elele m'ele*—"to arms, to arms"—in the dead of night.[10] The city was enclosed by a thick five-foot-high mud wall fronted by a deep, four-foot-wide ditch. The wall was fifteen miles in circumference, but in many places it had crumbled so badly that it would offer no barrier to attack. It was a city both larger and better fortified than any in

Dahomey, and its population may have been greater than all of Dahomey; some estimated it at 300,000, but that was probably excessive. During the past year, the British had shipped thousands of muskets and seven cannon to the Egba. Already, the cannon were rusted, their carriages useless, but the army that awaited the Dahomeans was at least 15,000 men strong, each man armed with a musket.

As the Dahomean army, led by General Akati, approached Abeokuta early in 1851, it first attacked the town of Ishagga, twelve miles to the west of Abeokuta. Its ruler, Bakoko, eagerly surrendered, declaring his hatred of the Egba and offering to lead the Dahomean army to the weakest point along the walled city. Surreptitiously, however, he sent a warning to Abeokuta. Strangely gullible, Akati and his officers believed Bakoko. They were so overconfident that they did not even bother to scout the wall, nor attack in the predawn darkness. Bakoko convinced them that the Egba were on full alert at night because they expected the Dahomeans to attack in the dark, but that the men were asleep during the day.[11] Bakoko's men led the Dahomeans first to what proved to be the deepest point in the River Ogun, which had to be crossed to reach the city. As they forded it, cursing, the Dahomeans lost much of their gunpowder. Still, they drove back Abeokuta's army, most of whom then retreated to take up positions behind the city's wall. Next, the Dahomeans were guided to the strongest point of the Egba defense, unaware that in other places the wall had crumbled and effective defense there would have been very difficult.[12]

Attacking at noon, for six terrible hours Dahomey's 6,000 Amazons and 10,000 male soldiers threw themselves at the city wall time after time. As a British Christian missionary looked on through his telescope at the wall "black with people," as he said, and other British missionaries and their wives prayed fervently, an American missionary who had formerly been a Texas Ranger exhorted the Egba to fight harder while he blazed away at the Dahomeans with his rifle. The Egba did not need his help; they unleashed a devastating barrage of gunfire that time after time decimated the Dahomean ranks. Ten full-scale charges were beaten back.[13] Still, all who saw the battle agreed that the Amazons were magnificent. Their bodies glistening with palm oil so that no one could effectively grapple with them, many Amazons managed to climb the walls before being shot down. No Dahomean male soldiers appear to have joined them. A few women warriors actually fought their way into the city before they, too, were killed. Popular British military historian John Laffin has written that large numbers of Amazons entered the city, forming up ranks before being wiped out. He cited no source, and none of the eyewitness accounts mention anything like this.[14]

Those Amazons who were captured continued to resist, two of them killing Egba women who brought them food. In return, many prisoners were killed, and if the missionaries had not interceded on their behalf, all the Amazon prisoners would have been killed.[15] After the Dahomean army finally withdrew, between 1,200 and 1,600 Amazons lay dead outside the city's wall.[16] At least that number had been wounded, many to die later.[17] As the Dahomean army retreated, the Egba pursued, killing thousands more and wounding many others. Apparently as an act of revenge, the retreating Dahomean troops were said to have beheaded forty or so Ishaggan captives, including two women and a child.[18] When the fighting ended, the Dahomean army was decimated. Among the dead was General Akati.

Although the story may be apocryphal, it was widely reported that when the firing stopped at Abeokuta, Egba warriors ventured among the slain Dahomeans to carry out their traditional victory mission—cutting off the heads and genitals of the dead to be presented to their commander and king. Only then did they realize that most of the dead were women. Profoundly insulted that they had been assaulted by women soldiers, the Egba attacked the retreating Dahomeans with renewed fervor.[19] Egba women traditionally supported their male soldiers with food, drink, and encouragement, but they did not fight. For the Egba, war was man's work, and the martial spirit of the Amazons must have been perplexing. A few years later, when British army captain A. T. Jones went to Abeokuta to drill its army, he addressed the men, saying that he wanted to see if "they would fight like men or like women."[20] Perhaps he did not know about Dahomey's women warriors, or perhaps he knew only too well that they, too, fought like men.

In 1862, a rebuilt Dahomean army sought revenge by moving secretly against the town of Ishagga and its now prosperous leader, King Bakoko, whose treachery they had not forgotten. Attacking at dawn, they quickly overwhelmed the town and killed Bakoko, whose skull became a bowl from which new King Glele would often drink. Thousands of Ishaggans were captured, bound, and treated brutally as they were marched to the coast, where many were slaughtered. Missionaries led by Father Borghero successfully intervened to spare some of the children, who, along with their surviving parents, were sold into slavery.[21] Ishagga had been punished, but Abeokuta remained.

As the year 1864 began, King Glele told anyone who would listen that he was prepared to avenge his late father's defeat at Abeokuta thirteen years earlier. He told Burton that "this year Abeokuta must be as a mouse before a cat," inviting him to join the campaign and "sit behind the army to see the sport."[22] Burton declined, warning the new king that without better artillery, the Dahomean army could not hope to breach Abeokuta's walls, but Glele led his army to war nonetheless.[23] With three gunpowder stripes painted on his face, wearing all black, and carrying a nail-studded war club, he rode toward Abeokuta determined to have revenge. Forewarned, just as they had been in 1851, the Egba repaired Abeokuta's walls and ditches while Egba villages along the Dahomean line of march were evacuated and all food was removed from the fields. The rebuilt Dahomean army left Abomey on February 22, marching from 6 A.M. to 2 P.M. one day and resting the next, as they covered 120 miles at a pace of 10 miles per daily march. This was hardly a breakneck pace, but the need to forage for food slowed them, as they ranged widely in search of anything to relieve their hunger because they carried only enough dried beans, parched rice, onions, and roasted palm nuts to sustain themselves for a few days.

The army consisted of only about 11,000 men and women, and 5,000 of these were noncombatant carriers who struggled with their loads of supplies and dragged three brass six-pound cannons, the only artillery Dahomey had. One was marked "Mexico, 1815," and the other two were inscribed "Seville, 1805."[24] The tall, copper-skinned King Glele, with perpetually bloodshot eyes and mandarin-long fingernails, was thirsting for revenge, but he played no prominent part in the attack, which began on March 15, at 6:30 A.M. under cover of fog after the troops had downed their traditional generous ration of rum.[25] Despite poor visibility, the Dahomean troops were detected long before they reached Abeokuta's walls, and the Egba, already on the alert, quickly took their positions, opening fire with modern, British-provided cannon as well as thousands of muskets. The Dahomean army advanced to about 200 yards from the wall, where they halted to display their banners before their tall commander, dressed entirely in blue, gave the order to attack, and the troops—led by Amazons screaming, "Conquer or die"—sprinted toward the city, already shrouded in smoke. Some crouched in the ditch firing up at Egba riflemen, and others tried to crawl through tunnels in the walls, only to be decapitated as they poked their heads inside.

The brunt of the attack was once again borne by the Amazons, who climbed the wall, snatched away Egba muskets, and even threw large stones at the enemy. One woman lost her arm in the attack but shot an Egba with her other hand before being killed with a sword. Three Amazons actually planted their banners on the city's wall before being killed and dismembered, their heads and hands being paraded around the city on poles to the cheers of the defenders.[26] The only Dahomeans to get over the wall were four Amazons. One woman sat on the wall for some time smoking her pipe and contemptuously staring at the Egba before she was shot down.[27]

After an hour of combat, during which some eighty Dahomeans lost their lives at the wall, fifty or so more died before reaching the wall, and four Dahomean Amazons lay dead inside the wall, the army retreated out of range of Egba fire and sat down. After repelling a weak Egba attack, Glele's army began a slow, disorganized retreat until a large, previously unseen, Egba force fell on their rear, precipitating a rout. Officers tried to organize defensive stands, but the Egba were not to be stopped. At each stand, more Dahomeans were killed and more weapons lost, including their three brass cannons. When the rout ended that night, thirty-five miles west of Abeokuta, the Dahomean army had been shattered. As many as 2,000 prisoners had been taken, and at least that many had been killed.[28] The Egba claimed that the Dahomean loss was almost 7,000. The Egba loss in killed and wounded was very light. Although the Amazons had been defeated, their exceptional courage was noted by all who saw the battle.[29]

After the battle, as in the first attack of 1851, with the corps of Amazons virtually annihilated, the king was forced to conscript young Dahomean women to replace as many of the dead as possible. The Amazon battalions that were destroyed at Abeokuta had been made up mostly of women captured from other societies. Now, lacking enough slave women to replace them, King Glele would have to restock his army almost entirely with Dahomean women. Young women aged twelve to fourteen with powerful physiques were ideal candidates for induction into the badly depleted Amazon army, but many other women were apparently impressed into service because they were promiscuous or guilty of criminal acts or were young women whose parents simply could not control them.[30]

As the nineteenth century wore on, the Amazons would fight in more wars, including yet another failed assault on Abeokuta in 1871, but their greatest and final test would come against the French beginning in 1890. A photograph of Amazons taken in that year shows women ranging in age from the early twenties to middle age, some thin and attractive, others old, stout, and scowling.[31] These new Amazons would fight just as bravely and as well as their predecessors.

While Glele was mounting his failed campaigns against Abeokuta, France was slowly becoming the supreme European power on the Dahomean coast. The German sphere of influence was in Togo on Dahomey's western border, and Britain claimed what is now Nigeria to the east of Dahomey. With Portuguese influence waning, France began serious diplomatic negotiations with Dahomey as early as 1851, and in 1868 Glele ceded Cotonou to France. As a means of maintaining Dahomean control of this important trading center, Glele also installed a Fongbe speaker named Toffa as king of Porto Novo. To Glele's distress, however, the French became increasingly demanding of trading rights, and Toffa acted as if he were independent of Dahomey. Tension grew when Glele renounced his treaty obligations to France at the same time as the European powers met in Brussels in 1889–1890 to carve out spheres of influence over those parts of Africa that were still free of European dominion. In August 1889, Britain and France reached an accord over France's exclusive right to establish a protectorate over Dahomey, a right the Portuguese had waived two years earlier.

On October 1, 1889, French emissary Jean Bayol landed at Porto Novo with what amounted to unlimited powers to negotiate with King Glele. Bayol was a French naval physician, but he was above all an autocrat with an unshakable belief in the glory of France. Sporting a goatee and a large waxed mustache, he was much more inclined to make demands than he was to negotiate. Because he wanted to witness the "customs," by then notorious in European minds, Bayol delayed his trip to Abomey until mid-November, arriving on November 20 just in time to be welcomed by a large crowd waving, to his considerable annoyance, British flags, and to see what he referred to as "200 sacrifices." Bayol briefly met King Glele, delivering twenty-three gifts while the crowd shouted that the elderly frail king was the "lion of lions."[32]

Bayol quickly developed a loathing for Dahomey.[33] His temper did not improve when he was forced to wait a full week before being granted an audience with the "king," who turned out to be Glele's son, Prince Kondo, not King Glele. Not aware that Glele, then about seventy-five, was too ill to see anyone, Dr. Bayol became even more annoyed. After thirty-three days of frustration in Abomey, a bout of malaria, virtual house arrest, and no willingness to compromise on the part of Prince Kondo, Bayol returned to the coast, where he vengefully arrested some thirty Dahomean officials.

Kondo retaliated by taking nine European hostages, including the charismatic French priest Father Dogère. Roughly handled, the Europeans were chained by their necks to a cable and made to walk to Abomey in bare feet, the sun beating on their bare heads, with food and water nowhere to be seen. A few days later, on about December 29, 1889, King Glele died and was succeeded by his son, Prince Kondo, who took the title, King Béhanzin. Soon, the hostages' treatment improved, and they were even given an audience with King Béhanzin, who professed friendship with France, then released the prisoners.[34]

A few months later, about twenty so-called Amazons were exhibited in Paris, where, in full warlike regalia, they danced, chanted, and performed military gyrations. It is unlikely that any of these women had ever been Amazons—indeed ten were Egba—but under the sponsorship of a British entrepreneur, they went to France, then remained in Europe for two more years traveling to several cities; at least one member of the troupe is known to have died in Prague.[35] It is possible that they were impostors being used to create the impression that Dahomey favored French colonialism; audiences apparently received this idea from them.[36]

As Bayol was on his way to Dahomey, the French press began to print sensational accounts of Dahomean barbarism, with the need for French civilization made abundantly clear. This example is a description of Dahomean warfare by Paris's *Petit Journal:*

> The elders are killed; women are disembowelled and children still nursing are stoned. The young boys and girls are seized, bound and kept in reserve, the former for the slave trade and the latter for human sacrifice. Afterwards, the fields are deserted, crops ruined and houses destroyed. Such are the crimes committed by the king and his army of ferocious savages.[37]

On the outbreak of war in 1890, *Le Petit Parisien* produced numerous grisly drawings of bloody human sacrifice that, along with other press accounts describing Béhanzin as a "Tyrant," seem intended to provide ample justification for French intervention in Dahomey.[38]

After Bayol's return from Abomey to the coast, Béhanzin sent units of locally mustered militia plus a few regulars to the coast, apparently as a defensive measure. There were only a few hundred French soldiers and some African auxiliaries on the coast at this time, but they were armed with modern weapons the Dahomean soldiers had never faced before. Each man had an eight-shot, bolt-action Lebel rifle that rapidly fired new smokeless bullets with such velocity that they could penetrate a large tree and still kill a man standing behind it, something a French Foreign Legionnaire later witnessed.[39] This rifle was so efficient that it remained the principal weapon of the French army until 1939. The rifle was also equipped with a deadly two-foot-long bayonet. Because by this point in history the Dahomean troops no longer had bayonets, their basic tactic of charging ahead into hand-to-hand combat proved suicidal. Even worse for the Dahomean army, the French had machine guns like those that dominated fighting in World War I, and they also had modern breech-loading artillery, the famous French 75-millimeter cannon, noted for its accuracy and rapid-firing capabilities with high explosive shells. These artillery pieces were so effective that they remained in service during World War II. To counter this array of modern weaponry, the Dahomean troops had only their single-shot, muzzle-loading 1822-model muskets—many of which were defective—and an assortment of swords, razors, and clubs.[40]

In March 1890, at a place called Zogbo, near Cotonou, some 500 Dahomean militia drawn from nearby villages gathered in a wooded area almost a mile from a French detachment. Without waiting for the Dahomeans to take any action, French artillery and machine guns opened fire, followed by an infantry charge. The Dahomean militia briefly returned fire, then ran, leaving some of their dead and numerous old muskets behind them.[41] Some 300 Dahomeans lost their lives; the French had only 2 killed and 2 wounded. The French next arrested Dahomean officials in Cotonou.

In rapid response, King Béhanzin called for general mobilization. He also mustered all of his standing army. A French hostage who saw the army's encampment was awed by the "grandeur" of the force he estimated at nearly 20,000, 4,000 of them Amazons: "Old or young, ugly or pretty, they are marvelous to contemplate. As solidly muscled as the male soldiers, their attitude is as disciplined and as correct."[42] The Amazons rested under parasols, and when civilians pressed around them, they imperiously snapped "stay away."[43]

In early March 1890, a large Dahomean force attacked Cotonou before dawn, killing several French in outposts. Now fully alert, the French riddled the Dahomeans with cannon and machine-gun fire. A few Dahomean men almost broke through the French lines, as did some Amazons in another sector, but French bayonets drove them off with fearful losses, including numerous Amazons, one of whom was shot as she was about to behead a French corporal she had captured.[44] Horrified by these ferocious women, the French commander, Lieutenant-Colonel Terrillon , called the Amazons "les harpies."[45] Despite their losses and the coming of daylight, which made them even more vulnerable to French fire, the Dahomean troops fought until 10 A.M., several times forcing the French to retreat, before the Dahomeans broke off their attacks. At noon, chanting and drumming was heard in the French lines, and led by an officer on a horse, the Dahomeans attacked again, suffering terrible losses. As in earlier battles, most of the Dahomean musket fire went well over the heads of the French as the Dahomean troops continued to fire from the hip, usually while on the run. A French officer recalled "the terrible hand-to-hand fighting, the amazons, always in front, uttered their war cries and came to die at the feet of our men."[46]

On March 25, Dahomean troops reverted to guerrilla tactics, ambushing a French force and driving it back in retreat with substantial casualties. A French observer wrote of the Amazons, "They displayed an incredible relentlessness."[47] On April 16, at the battle of Atekoupa, King Béhanzin personally led 2,000 Amazons against reinforced French troops, and despite their great superiority in weapons, the French were forced to retreat to their fortifications at Porto Novo. Soon after this battle, the rains came, and the first Franco-Dahomean war ended. But the Amazons had made an impression on the French: "Their fury and their disdain for fear endowed all the Amazons with the terrible renown that has reached us in France."[48] A French officer wrote that they charged with "remarkable intrepidity and courage."[49] The same officer remembered being charged by an Amazon "roaring like a wild beast" before he killed her with a pistol shot to the head.[50]

Despite their severe losses, Dahomean morale remained surprisingly high, and the army moved north to raid Egba territory, razing ten towns and taking more than 1,000 prisoners.[51] As the army returned to Abomey with its captives and its battered legions, it was time to take stock of the threat posed by the now fully entrenched French on the coast. It is likely that Dahomean losses exceeded 2,000, whereas the French admitted to only 43 dead.[52] The disparity came about in part because the French had fought behind fortifications, whereas the Dahomeans had attacked over open ground; yet it was clear to Béhanzin and his military advisers that French weapons were so vastly superior that if Dahomey hoped to defend itself against the French invasion that seemed inevitable, the army would need to rearm itself with more modern weapons.

As the Dahomean arms buildup went forward, the French attempted to find a diplomatic solution. Their emissary was Father Dogère, a former hostage at Abomey whose charm and ability to speak Fongbe had made him popular with Béhanzin's court. When the young priest arrived in Abomey he was given a hero's welcome with a 100-gun salute, followed by some 10,000 gunshots and a military parade. Béhanzin listened to Father Dogère's peace proposals favorably, releasing thirty-five hostages and sending a delegation to the coast to continue negotiations. On October 30, 1890, a treaty was signed providing that King Béhanzin would respect the French protectorate over the Kingdom of Porto Novo and abstain from all incursions into the territories forming this kingdom. Béhanzin also recognized French treaty rights over Cotonou, for which France would pay him an annual compensation of 20,000

francs. There was no provision for the cessation of human sacrifices or any other social or religious reforms for Dahomey.[53]

While Dahomey engaged in diplomacy designed to buy time,
Béhanzin continued to seek out modern weapons. To no surprise
on the part of the French, German merchants at Whydah and on
the coast of Togo to the west proved only too happy to sell more-
or-less modern rifles and ammunition in return for slaves.
Although the transatlantic slave trade had been virtually at an end
for three decades, the slave trade was still practiced within Africa,
and Béhanzin traded several thousand newly captured slaves for
over 1,000 rapid-firing rifles including American Spencers and
Winchesters. Five shiploads of slaves found themselves on
German ships bound for German, Portuguese, and Belgian
colonies in Africa.[54] A Swiss firm sold the Dahomeans 3,000 muskets. Dahomey also bought six Krupp cannons, several machine
guns, and over 100,000 rounds of bullets and cannon shells from
German firms, and at least one German spent a month in Abomey
training Dahomeans in the use of these new weapons.[55] A considerable number of these weapons were not in good working order,
something the French gratefully noted, and hardly any of the cannon shells exploded when they were eventually fired. Still, this
arms trade so alarmed the French that they soon blockaded the
coast, although more arms nevertheless got through. But in a fate-
ful and inexplicable oversight, Béhanzin did not purchase bayonets. This error would cost him many lives and dramatically
shorten the war.

By late in the year of 1891, Dahomey's army had been largely
rearmed, and so many new recruits had been mobilized that
Béhanzin could field a force of about 15,000, perhaps 4,000 of
whom were women. The king began a series of raids south into
French-controlled portions of his kingdom, pillaging, burning,
and spreading panic among villagers who were collaborating
with the French. These were small-scale raids, and no large battles
were fought, but a convenient casus belli was seized upon by the
French when one of their gunboats sailed well north into
Dahomey and was fired upon. There were no casualties, but the

French were offended as only a colonial power could be. Following a vote of 301 to 177 in the Chamber of Deputies, France decided to send a formidable expeditionary force to Abomey to compel Béhanzin's obedience.

Under the command of a marine colonel, Alfred A. Dodds, over 3,000 French regulars assembled at Porto Novo, fifteen miles east of Cotonou. In addition to 76 French officers, about 1,000 of these men were French marines, half of them artillerymen. The remainder were either Hausa or Senegalese Africans, well equipped with modern weapons and thoroughly trained. The French troops were uniformed in white, complete with pith helmets; the African troops wore dark blue jackets and blue-tasseled hats. Most of the Africans fought barefooted, as did the Dahomean troops. The French also had a cavalry unit of 228 men, five heavily-armed gunboats that could navigate the Weme River, 2,239 porters, and 132 mules.[56] Dodds's officers referred to this army as a "tour de Babel" because its men spoke so many languages.[57]

On August 25, 1892, the spearhead of Dodds's force came ashore in the form of 800 French Foreign Legionnaires from Algeria. The king, Toffa, still well disposed to the French but always unpredictable, greeted them the next day when they marched into Porto Novo. The Legionnaires laughed heartily at the king because, although he sometimes dressed in great finery, this time, as a former British officer serving in the Legion reported, he was wearing "a French naval officer's cap, and a richly embroidered frock coat, but nothing else whatever . . ."[58]

The next day, the Legionnaires—generally considered among the finest infantry in the world—were surprised to see Colonel Dodds's light brown skin, a result of his mixed French and Senegalese ancestry. But they were encouraged by his correct military bearing, his medals, and his reputation. Fifty years old, a graduate of Saint-Cyr, France's prestigious military academy, and a veteran of campaigns in Senegal and Indochina, Dodds would prove to be a capable leader. After being outfitted in lightweight uniforms and supplied with quinine, the Legionnaires began to slog up the left bank of the River Weme, following the main force that had gone on ahead. Dodds chose to advance along this seemingly difficult route to avoid the barricades and entrenched artillery the Dahomeans had placed along the traditional route to Abomey, and to take advantage of supporting fire from his gunboats that would accompany him north up the River Weme. The Legionnaires, many of them non-French, including many Germans and Alsatians and even a Russian nobleman, would serve as both the advance and the rear guard of Dodds's force. Despite their previous service in Algeria, they found the heat exhausting.

On the morning of September 19, 1892, Dahomean troops attacked without warning at a place called Dogba, driving the French back until the Legionnaires counterattacked them in a ferocious bayonet charge, stabbing Dahomean men and women one after another, then throwing them off to the side "like a farmer pitching hay," as one of them later said. Although the Dahomean soldiers, women as well as men, had repeated their failed tactic of frontal attack, they now added a new threat by sending Amazon sharpshooters into tall trees to fire down on the exposed French. A French marine commander was killed along with several other officers before the snipers could be shot out of the trees. A French officer was impressed by the deadly accuracy with which the Amazons fired their modern rifles.[59]

During the course of more than three hours of fighting, a sergeant major of the Senegalese Spahis (cavalry) was surrounded by Amazons, captured, and taken away. When his body was later found by a scouting party, it was clear that he had been tortured to death, castration being but one horror among many that he had suffered.[60] There was also evidence that parts of him had been cooked and apparently eaten. In retaliation, two Amazon prisoners—one described as an attractive, pleasant teenager who denied wrongdoing—were executed by order of Colonel Dodds. After the battle, the French counted 825 Dahomean bodies, most of them Amazons. One Legionnaire later wrote that of the three Amazons his men had killed, two "seemed very young, 14 or 15 years old; they were very beautiful, strongly muscled, but finely too; the third was old, her face crossed with scars, she must have led a squad."[61] Another Legionnaire described dead Amazons he saw as "very young girls, hardly formed," but there were also "old women with flaccid breasts"; an old and young woman who lay dead together seemed to him to be mother and daughter.[62] A third Legionnaire wrote in his journal that he could not stop shaking as he looked down at what he described as the peaceful but "mildly reproachful" expressions of the dead Dahomean women.[63] Because cremation was easier than burial for the heat-exhausted French, many of the bodies were soaked in kerosene and set on fire.[64] However, most of the dead were only lightly singed, and large piles of naked, charred bodies were left as a ghastly reminder of the carnage.

After some bloody but small-scale skirmishes dominated by French machine-gun fire, the next major battle took place on October 4, when Dodds's force marched closer to Abomey. At 9 A.M., the advance guard of two squadrons of Senegalese cavalry were attacked so furiously that they retreated in "great disorder." Next, a company of Hausas broke in a similar rout. A Legionnaire described what happened next:

> The turn of the Senegalese tirailleurs (skirmishers) came next. A battalion of Amazons attacked them and gave them a very rough time indeed, but the tirailleurs stood their ground until reinforced by some Marine Infantry. Anyone inclined to sympathise with the Amazons on account of their sex, and look upon the combat between them and our men as unequal, may take it from me that their sympathy would be misplaced. These young women were far and away the best men in the Dahomeyan army, and woman to man were quite a match for any of us. They were armed with Spencer repeating carbines, and made much better use of them than the men made of their rifles; and for work at close quarters they had a small heavy-backed chopping sword or knife, very much like a South American machete, with which they did great execution. They fought like unchained demons, and if driven into a corner did not disdain the use of their teeth and nails. One of them was seized and disarmed by a Marine Infantryman in this fight, but she was so far from being beaten that

she at once turned on her captor and set about biting his nose off. The man yelled out for his mother, but the lady would not leave off worrying him until she was cut down by the sword of Lieutenant Toulouse who rushed to the man's assistance. Toulouse would be killed in battle a short time later.[65]

Another legionnaire wrote:

> The uniform of these female warriors was a sort of kilted divided skirt of blue cotton stuff. This garment barely reached to the knees. It was supported at the waist by a leather belt which carried the cartridge pouches. The upper part of their bodies were [sic] quite nude, but the head was covered with a coquettish red fez, or tarboosh, into which was stuck an eagle's feather. These ladies were all exceedingly well developed, and some of them were very handsome.[66]

Some of the French believed that the Amazons' courage was inspired by gin, and there is ample evidence that these warrior women had long enjoyed alcohol, especially on the morning before battle:

> These female warriors fought with extraordinary courage, always in the lead, setting an example to the others by their fearlessness. Before the battle, they had got drunk on English gin, working themselves up to an indescribable state of frenzy. The mass of empty bottles we found afterwards was irrefutable proof of this fact.[67]

According to an anonymous Legionnaire's journal, several Amazons were taken prisoner. Although the French were repelled by their shaved heads, their teeth filed to sharp points, and the human skulls that some wore tied around their waists, they agreed that the women's bodies were magnificent—powerful but sensual and graceful. They smelled of sweat, dried blood, and palm oil, and they were caked with dust, but for one Legionnaire, at least, this only enhanced their attractiveness. The French gave the women water and bandaged their wounds while discussing what they should do with them. Through a translator, the Amazons were asked if they knew what would happen to them now. One matter-of-factly ventured that the French would rape them, then kill them. When a French sergeant firmly denied this, several women argued animatedly before saying that rather than going to prison they would become slaves to the French, but their leader, apparently an officer, rejected this option saying that the women would choose Legionnaires as their husbands.

In response, the French chattered loudly before their sergeant ordered quiet. He told the Dahomeans that Legionnaires could not marry during active service and that, in any event, Frenchmen chose their wives, women did not choose them. He concluded by telling the women to be "peaceful" and they would be taken care of. In fact, they were fed and treated well, being allowed to bathe nude in a nearby pond. Quickly, the women visibly softened, one even beckoning to some Legionnaires to join them. Those Legionnaires who watched them bathe "always insisted that they were among the loveliest women on earth."[68] Within a matter of days, these women warriors, who had so often insisted that they were men, had seemingly become "women," and attractive ones at that, who fussed over their appearance and flirted with the Legionnaires, who, in turn, admired their beauty and became protective of them. These Amazon captives were young women who had apparently not yet fully "become men." They were not only pretty but helpful, too, carrying some of the Legionnaires' gear all the way to Abomey, just as Dahomean women might be expected to do for their men.[69] It should go without saying that older Amazons would not have been seen as "attractive," nor is it likely that such experienced warriors would so readily have reverted to "feminine" roles.

Despite withering French fire, the Dahomean troops—men and women both—persisted in their suicidal attacks time after time until they were finally compelled to break off contact. At this point, the French attacked, and despite the great advantage their bayonets gave them, they were driven back several times. Throughout the battle, Dahomean artillery dropped shell after shell into the French lines, but only rarely did any of these faulty shells explode. The accuracy of Dahomean artillery fire was so great that the French could not believe that the guns were being handled by inexperienced

Africans. Apparently some of them were not, because three Germans and a Belgian were captured and accused of commanding the guns. All four were summarily executed by Dodds's order.[70]

After two hours of attack and counterattack, Senegalese cavalry finally broke through to the Dahomean artillery and sabered the gunners. At this point, the surviving Dahomean troops retreated in great haste, and the French were unable to pursue effectively. The Dahomeans still consistently fired high, and most proved to be armed with obsolete weapons. For example, a French captain picked up an old musket left on the battlefield only to gasp in astonishment. This was the same weapon he had personally used as a sergeant in the Franco-Prussian War twenty-two years earlier. It still had his serial number stamped on it.[71]

By this point, King Béhanzin's army was on the verge of collapse, but it continued to fight the advancing French in a series of holding actions. On October 6, 1892, only 17 of more than 400 Amazons who fought in these battles survived.[72] The French were suffering, too, with the numbers of wounded and sick mounting, and with thirst so extreme that men would ignore Dahomean fire to fill their canteens at any of the few available sources. Throngs of mosquitoes also tormented them. By now, it was plain to the French that the Amazons were in authority over the male Dahomean troops, as they could be seen exhorting the men to greater efforts, and great bravery was actually forthcoming as the Dahomeans used the cover of thick brush to stop the advance of the French and to prevent them from quenching their thirst. One Amazon led by example, advancing to within a few dozen paces of the officer commanding the Legion at that time and shooting him in the chest: "The bravery and the military skill of these women soldiers filled us all with admiration, and we were pretty well agreed that if the whole of the Dahomeyan army had been made up of them it would have taken a much larger force than ours to have got to Abomey."[73]

An anonymous Legionnaire's diary describes the French ordeal:

Three times our bayonet charges threw the enemy back. Lieutenant D'Urbal, who was a most brilliant officer, was wounded in the arm; Sergeant-Major Vabray, hit in the shoulder, collapsed beside him.

Men began to fall like flies. Karl and François, two of my platoon mates, were killed; the former was a Danish engineer, the latter a Belgian. Old Guenal, a real old sweat from 1870, was wounded. The ambulance was exposed to the burning sun, and the only shelter for our wounded consisted of a few banana-palm leaves and tufts of grass. In the evening, the Colonel, realizing how exposed we were, ordered us to fall back on Apka. It was a three-hour march. We arrived exhausted and again tortured by thirst. We chewed grass, licked stones, even our rifle butts. When we tried to snatch a few hours sleep, we were eaten alive by mosquitoes and huge red ants which invaded our uniforms to reach our flesh.[74]

Only ten miles from Abomey but unable to advance and desperate for water, Dodds ordered a retreat in search of water, which his cavalry found just in time to avert disaster. His army exhausted, and many of the Europeans down with dysentery, Dodds fortified his camp and sent for every available man from the coast. While waiting for help to arrive, water parties had to walk well over a mile to a well. One party was unexpectedly cut off and surrounded:

We hardly expected to see any of them attempt to break through the enemy to get to us, and we were therefore surprised, and it must be confessed somewhat amused, to see an unarmed legionary sprinting towards us with a gigantic Dahomeyan close at his heels. The nigger was armed with one of the heavy-backed short swords, which I have previously described as being very much like a Cuban machete, and every now and again he would race up close to the legionary and make a cut at his head. But every time he did this the legionary must have heard his approach, for no sooner was the machete raised in the air than our comrade would put on a desperate spurt and draw away again. It was a real sporting sprint-race, with a man's life for the prize, and it was so interesting that both we and the enemy temporarily stopped firing to watch it. The legionary won by a short head, so to say, the gallant black pursuing him right up to the muzzles of our rifles and meeting his death at the hands of a Senegalese Tirailleur who was devoid of the sporting instinct.[75]

Soon after this "sport," French reinforcements arrived with ample supplies, and Dodds resumed his march on Abomey. Just as the advance was getting under way, Dahomeans waving large white flags approached, requesting permission to speak to Colonel Dodds. Béhanzin declared himself willing to accept French protection, but Dodds's troops would have to return to the coast. Dodds categorically rejected this proposal, countering that Béhanzin must cede the entire seaboard to France, abolish slavery and human sacrifice, pay 15 million francs, surrender eight Krupp cannons and 2,000 quick-firing rifles, turn over three important persons as hostages, and permit French troops to occupy Abomey. Béhanzin was given twenty-four hours to comply. Just before the deadline expired, Dahomean emissaries turned over two cannons, 100 rifles, 5,000 francs, and two hostages, with a promise to pay the remainder. Béhanzin also sent a well-crafted silver finger, symbolizing his wish to cooperate as if part of the same hand.[76] Spurning these gestures, Dodds marched on.

Half an hour later the French were attacking again against little resistance, only to discover to their surprise that the Dahomeans were still full of fight. The next day, the French attacked again against what one French Foreign Legionnaire called the "toughest bit of fighting we had yet come across."[77] Time and again, the French charged only to be driven back. Later in the day, the Dahomeans were finally overpowered in a battle in which it is estimated that they lost 2,500 men and women to about 100 French.[78] The Amazons did not die without a fight. They were ferocious, swinging their swords, even biting and scratching—literally fighting "tooth and nail"—as they wrestled for their lives. As before, many may have been fueled by the English gin that had earlier filled many bottles found at the battle scene, and a few Amazons were found in a drunken stupor. When these women were later interrogated, they refused to reveal any information of value to the French.[79] All the Foreign Legionnaires who wrote about these battles praised the Amazons' courage. One wrote:

> We were attacked by a body of the enemy some thousands strong, and we formed into company squares to resist their onslaught. As at

Dogba (an earlier battle) our fire literally mowed down the advancing lines, but they came on again and again in the most determined manner, and there is no doubt in my mind that if they had been under capable European leadership we would have found ourselves in the very queerest of queer streets. As it was, they were compelled at last to retire to their entrenchments; but when we followed them and stormed the earthworks at the point of the bayonet they drove us back again and again.[80]

The battle lasted for ten hours.

The next morning, what remained of the Dahomean army attacked and once again drove back the French, but after nearly a full day of often hand-to-hand combat, the Dahomean army finally broke and melted away. Soon after, the French resumed their advance, their artillery blasting everything in their path, only to face still-determined Amazons who attacked them again and again outside the town of Cana. The women not only threw themselves into combat but also taunted the Dahomean men to join them. The Amazons fought with such valor that they repeatedly forced the French to form a defensive square formation in order to fight them off. Once again, many artillery shells fell among the French but none exploded.[81] The battle had been raging continuously since 5 A.M., and by 2 P.M., the French were faint from their exertions under a blazing sun without food or water. Suddenly, and for no apparent reason, the Dahomeans literally ran away in unison, as if executing a planned maneuver. Apparently, King Béhanzin had ordered the withdrawal, and he led the remains of his army back toward Abomey, bypassing the heavily fortified town of Cana. Its garrison leaderless and with no more taste for a fight, the Dahomeans abandoned the city, which Dodds promptly put to the torch.

The Amazons also abandoned several of their war camps, including one described by the French. Around a large, open-sided structure apparently used for meetings and another large domicile for the king, there were hundreds of shelters for the soldiers. A French officer wrote, "In general, these shelters are very carefully constructed and much more comfortable than the best tents. The whole camp is irreproachably clean . . . without the least garbage around the huts."[82] Another French officer was also impressed by the structures that he saw, praising "the delicacy and originality of their shapes and the graceful meticulousness of the tiniest details. These gems of shelters must have been the Amazons' quarters. They had built them with their own hand, because men would not have achieved such perfection. . . . We were amazed at this resourcefulness."[83]

After resting his men in Cana for several days while waiting for resupply, Dodds ordered the town burned to the ground and then led his army toward Abomey on the same fine, thirty-yard-wide grassy road bordered by beautiful, large trees that earlier European visitors had admired. It was truly a royal road and much appreciated by the French. After seven miles, Dodds halted on a rise that overlooked Abomey a mile in the distance. As the French force paused, an envoy from Béhanzin arrived waving a white flag. What he said to Dodds, by then promoted to general, is not known, but it was rumored that he came to say that since Dodds had burned Cana, Béhanzin would save him the trouble of burning Abomey by doing so himself, and as the French looked on, smoke began to rise from the large city. In reality, Béhanzin ordered the city burned so that the French could not make use of it.[84] What these emissaries actually attempted to do was purchase peace with an offer of cash and other valuables. Dodds scornfully dismissed them.

By the time Dodds's men reached the city, it was engulfed in flames. The French did not see a single Dahomean in Abomey, but they found ample stores of liquor and ammunition, although no treasure. While French troops quartered themselves in what remained of King Béhanzin's skull-festooned palace, the king became a fugitive in the north, moving from village to village with a small retinue for more than a year before being captured. How many Dahomeans were killed or wounded in this war will never be known, but the Amazons were virtually annihilated. Only fifty or sixty were thought to have survived.[85] The French suffered 27 percent battle casualties, including forty-five officers. Nearly 75 percent of their force was incapacitated by disease for some part of the campaign.[86] The original Foreign Legion battalion of 800 men was reinforced by 250 men during the campaign. Of these 1,050 men, only 450 lived to return to Algeria. The majority died of fever.[87]

Béhanzin surrendered on January 25, 1894, his hiding place betrayed by his brother, Goutchili, who would replace him as king. Carried to Abomey in an iron cage on wheels, Béhanzin proved to be a tall, light-skinned man with a mild manner who so constantly smoked a long chased-silver pipe that, like his ancestors, he had to be followed at all times by a woman with a spittoon. He was exiled to Martinique with four of his wives and their children, along with a Dahomean prince, his wife, and an interpreter.[88] French authorities treated them graciously. But to his dying day, Béhanzin could not believe that the French had refused to accept his offer of money to end the war, something the Oyo had once been happy to do.[89] Transferred from Martinique to Algeria, he died there in 1906 without seeing Dahomey again.

The French authorities appointed Béhanzin's brother, who took the name Ago-li-Agbo, as the new king. A handful of the few surviving Amazons were allowed to serve him as royal guards, but the Dahomean army, including the surviving Amazons, was disbanded. Without access to money or other forms of wealth, the new king was powerless. When the French deposed him in 1900, his royal treasury amounted to 200 francs.[90] Some of Dahomey's surviving Amazons married, but most proved to be infertile, perhaps as a result of their prolonged use of herbal contraceptives as required by their officers. Their married lives proved to be turbulent, as one might expect. They were inclined to quarrel with cowives, often becoming violent as a French administrator noted. He also observed that married Amazons were known for their use of a "certain warlike temper" against their husbands.[91] Other Amazons refused to marry at all, insisting that they were superior to men, and that marriage would mean servitude to men.[92]

Paintings of Amazons were displayed in ethnographic exhibitions in Paris in 1891 attended by nearly 1 million people. The

Amazons were described as "for the most part young and pretty
. . . in their own way."[93] Another exhibition in Paris in 1893 was
visited by 2.7 million people. In that same year, a similar exhibition
appeared at the Chicago World's Fair. During the Paris exhibition
of 1893, Dahomeans and Frenchmen were pitted in a race requir-
ing them to carry a sixty-kilogram weight nonstop for 100 kilometers. Forty-two Frenchmen and ten Dahomeans competed in the
race; a Dahomean finished ten kilometers ahead of the second-
place Frenchman, becoming a press sensation as a result.[94] In 1900,
the Paris World's Fair attracted 50 million people, the largest number ever to attend such an exhibition. There was a Dahomey pavilion featuring a "tower of sacrifices," consisting of a pike supporting "actual skulls of slaves executed before the eyes of Behanzin,"
according to the guide book provided for visitors.[95]

As time passed, these former soldiers had little influence on
Dahomean society except as mythologized heroines of the past,
but in 1969, and perhaps on other occasions as well, the court was
treated to singing, dancing, and military formations by a group of
women dressed as soldiers. Amazons entered the popular culture
of cinema and television as voluptuous, eroticized women warriors from some legendary past. Like Tarzan and Jane, whom they
were made to resemble, they became fantasy characters, not heroines of precolonial history.[96]

In 1934, British anthropologist Geoffrey Gorer met a woman in
Abomey said to be a former Amazon officer; she was spinning
cotton:

There was something very pathetic and romantic about this battered
old relic of a completely dead age; she who had once proudly
boasted that she was no woman, but a man, was now reduced to the
degradation of spinning; she who had once captured her own booty
with her musket and cutlass was happy for a few sous to hobble into
the sun and be photographed. She must have been well over eighty.[97]

5

Gender Hierarchies
and Women in War

The women warriors of Dahomey confront us with a daunting puzzle. Why did their society make them the elite warriors of a highly successful professional army when no other society appears to have done the same thing? There is no easy answer
to this question. It is tempting to suggest that part of the explanation may be related to the fact that in comparison with other societies known to the ethnographic or historical record, Dahomey
gave women an impressive array of rights. Throughout their child-
hood and adolescent years, girls seem to have been as happy and
as well treated as boys. When they reached marriageable age, they
had the right to reject any husband proposed to them in favor of
another man of their choice. And as we have seen, should their
marriage not prove satisfactory, they had the right to divorce, but
husbands had no right to divorce their wives.

Women had the right to inherit property from their mothers, and
sometimes from their fathers as well, and they had the right to determine who should inherit their own property. Their property included money earned from their sales in various markets, as well
as gifts, farm animals, and even land. Some became wealthy. As
we have seen, some women had great political influence, and there

is evidence that they made decisions that were publicly carried out by male officeholders. Sometimes, they were not merely doubles for male officials, they held high office themselves. In addition to the many women who served as army officers outranking their male counterparts, they sometimes served as lineage heads, judges, and even village chiefs. They also held prestigious religious offices. This is an extraordinary record of equality, or near equality, in many important domains of life. Why, then, should they not have the right to serve in the army?

The difficulty with this explanation is that until well into the nineteenth century, the great majority of the Amazons were not Dahomean women at all; they were slaves taken from other societies. What is more, as we saw earlier, despite the rights of Dahomean women, Dahomean men felt superior to women in many ways and tended to dominate them in everyday life, if not always in public affairs. An ordinary Dahomean woman's lot in life included a great deal of hard work, even drudgery. Women dominated the palace, but men dominated the countryside. And in a final, telling irony, when women did become Amazons, they insisted that they were no longer women, that they had become men. To complicate matters even further, near equality in relations between men and women has occurred elsewhere without leading to the establishment of an elite female military force or, indeed, to any female participation in warfare at all. Moreover, the most entitled, powerful women in Dahomey—ministers, "doubles," lineage heads, or members of the royal lineage—did not become soldiers, and neither, apparently, did their daughters.

More satisfactory explanations of Dahomean women's service as elite soldiers appear to lie elsewhere. First, as noted earlier, once a system is created in which men may not enter a king's palatial domain after sunset, only women can guard him. This happened in several parts of West Africa, including the Kingdom of Whydah, which Dahomey so easily conquered. In most parts of West Africa, these female palace guards were not particularly warlike; much less were they elite soldiers. But if these women guards prove to be so loyal that they risk death to defend their king, and when they have great martial skills, the practice is likely to maintain itself, especially when women, such as captive slave women with no ties within Dahomey, found it easy to be wholly loyal to their king, who rewarded and even indulged them. Over the years, women palace guards in Dahomey perfected their military skills along with their intense loyalty, which was rewarded in many ways, as we have seen.

We have reviewed at length how young "Amazons" were selected, trained, rewarded, and made to feel that they had become not only "men", but men who were much superior to male soldiers wherever they might be found. This process of indoctrination and training was superbly effective, but it does not explain the transition of women from palace guards to the elite troops of Dahomey's conquering army. It seems likely that they had simply convinced King Gezo of their martial skills along with their loyalty, but it has been suggested that this transition became necessary because of a shortage of men. Many Dahomean men must have died in the kingdom's incessant wars. Moreover, because male slaves were more desirable to slave owners in the New World than females, substantially more men than women were sold overseas, leaving a sizable gender imbalance in Dahomey as early as the late eighteenth century. By the nineteenth century, it may have reached an imbalance of as few as 50 or so men to 100 women, possibly creating the need to recruit women as soldiers because relatively few men were available.[1] How important a factor this may have been in the creation of "Amazons" as a military elite is difficult to estimate, for it is obvious that if women had not proven their ability to excel as soldiers, they would never have achieved a preeminent place in the Dahomean military despite this apparent gender imbalance.

It is not known whether the emergence of the Amazons as Dahomey's best soldiers was a product solely of Gezo's leadership or of something that had more widespread support by Dahomean men. As far as the historical record permits us to know, Dahomean men made no organized protest against the rights and powers possessed by Dahomean women, although by the mid-nineteenth century male soldiers were clearly envious of the Amazons, and many other men were fearful of the powers of the king's wives and the powerful female officials. There is no record of public protest about women's rights and only one known public complaint about them (involving their participation in mutual-aid groups). Nor did Dahomean men openly inveigh against Dahomean women to European visitors, although they occasionally hinted their dissatisfaction, sometimes remarking on their own superiority. Still, it seems likely that many men, and perhaps most, resented some of the powers held by women, feared what women might say to the king about them, and wished for a world more openly dominated by males. And there is clear evidence that some senior male army officers resented the dominance and arrogance of the Amazons.

Dahomean men seem to have accepted the cosmological principle that the universe requires a balance between male and female forces, but in everyday life, ambivalence about women and their power sometimes spilled over into marital conflict. Of course, how men felt about the power held by their mothers, their sisters, and their daughters was likely to be far more positive than their feelings about their wives or unrelated women, especially the arrogant royal women. But perhaps the true feelings of most Dahomean men toward women in general can be seen in their reaction to the governmental changes initiated by the French after their conquest was completed in 1894. As was the common practice of European colonial governments, French officials imposed their own beliefs about the place of women in public life on the Dahomeans. They believed that women should confine themselves to being mothers and housewives, not hold high political office or greatly influence the affairs of government. In no time at all, Dahomey's government became all male. Neither Frenchwomen nor Dahomean women would take any major role in overseeing Dahomey's transition from independence to a French colony. There is no record of Dahomean men registering protests about this change in their way of governance. On the contrary, there is some evidence to suggest that many men were pleased by this change in Dahomey's government and in the gender hierarchy.[2]

To understand the dominance of the Amazons, we need to examine the history of gender inequality and the role of women as warriors over the course of human evolution. When women are relatively equal to men, are they more likely to engage in warfare? The topic of gender inequality, or "hierarchy" as some scholars now prefer, has generated a large and often controversial body of writing. Heated disagreements about the extent and causes of gender inequities continue to appear in scholarly journals as well as more popular writing (not to mention on the Internet), but something of a scholarly consensus has emerged. Even though women have wielded great power as monarchs in several parts of the world, it is generally agreed that no society has ever existed in which women in general dominated men in public affairs. There are some societies, like that of Dahomey, in which women and men were more or less equal in many ways, if not all, but as we have seen, there are also societies in which men have clearly dominated women, sometimes cruelly so.

Male prerogatives have included wife beating, which has taken place and has been approved of by men—in all but a handful of the world's small-scale societies. Men in such societies have also often monopolized the prized foods, as the Chukchee men of Eastern Siberia did, saying, "Being women, eat crumbs."[3] There has been psychological dominance, too. Among the horticultural Kamba of Kenya, women were frequently told that they had "small, smooth brains" and therefore could not think for themselves. Kamba men also openly boasted, "We buy them, we sell them—they are just like cattle."[4] Women in societies like these did not become warriors.

Yet this kind of extreme male dominance has been by no means universal. Women have had considerable political and economic power in many parts of the world, particularly in more complex societies such as kingdoms. In West Africa, for example, women sometimes had great influence over men, including their kings, and in some societies throughout Africa, the Middle East, and Asia, women did more than influence men; they became monarchs with autocratic powers. Before Islam changed the way Arab women were allowed to behave, the famous Bedouin queen Bat Zabbai (or Zenobia, as the Romans called her) held off the Romans for years by fighting at the head of Arab troops. Women also had prestige and power in some small-scale societies. The Cheyenne of the North American Plains, for example, allowed women such political power that George Bird Grinnell concluded that until recent times, women "had the final authority in camp."[5] They were also usually well treated by men and loved by their husbands, although, paradoxically it seems, they could be punished severely for adultery. Despite their power in society, they did not become soldiers.

Male dominance and oppression have been widespread realities of life around the world, but they have varied greatly in form and intensity and are easily misconstrued by outside observers. Equality and dominance are complex matters, and relations between men and women are very often far more complicated, and balanced, than they seem to outsiders. It is true that most small-scale societies around the world reserved hunting and dangerous activities such as war for men, but once again, this was not universal. Some women among the Plains Indians not only hunted buffalo and bear but also went to war. Women also went to war in many parts of Polynesia and Micronesia. And even in societies where women did not take part in war, they sometimes took more risks than men. In Tasmania, for example, as described in 1802 by Francois Péron—probably the first person to call himself an anthropologist—the men were remarkably indolent, seldom bestirring themselves except now and then to hunt wallabies or kangaroos—more a sport than an economic activity, as they were seldom successful at it. They also occasionally raided their neighbors, hoping to capture young women. But every day, Tasmanian women fetched heavy loads of water and wood, dove into deep and dangerous coastal waters to collect shellfish, swam offshore to club seals to death, and climbed very tall trees to kill possums. Despite taking all these risks—often while pregnant—and gathering virtually all the food in the Tasmanian diet, women were denied the choicest foods and were often beaten, things they complained bitterly about to European visitors.[6]

The smallest, simplest societies known to have existed are those that subsisted by hunting, gathering, or, sometimes, fishing. In general, these societies had a fair measure of equality between men and women. The Mbuti Pygmies of Zaire's tropical forest, the !Kung of the Kalahari Desert, and the Inuit, or Eskimo, are examples of small-scale societies in which women have traditionally made valued contributions to their society's subsistence and have usually enjoyed high status. There have been exceptions, to be sure, as the moving life story of Nisa, a !Kung woman who endured painfully troubled relations with men, so poignantly demonstrates.[7] There were also some small hunting-and-gathering societies in which women were subjected to brutal punishment and forced to carry out almost all of the difficult and dangerous work. As noted earlier, the Tasmanians had such a society, and on the Australian mainland, during much of the nineteenth century, Tiwi men so dominated women that husbands had the right to kill their wives with impunity. In societies like these, women did not go to war.

A range of women's rights is also found in horticultural societies. In some, like the Hopi or the Iroquois, women had considerable stature, but in others, there was marked gender inequality. In a good many small horticultural societies, women were clearly subservient to men. Highland New Guinea provides many examples, as does Latin America. Men among the Yanomami Indians of Venezuela's tropical forest were notorious not only for their perpetual warfare, aimed at capturing women, but also for their mistreatment of their wives. It is worth noting that there is no record of a society in which women raided their neighbors to capture men. And among the Fore of Highland Papua New Guinea, men denied animal flesh (principally pork) to women and children; choice foods were for men only, a common pattern in many parts of the world. Fore women and children supplemented their protein-poor diets by eating the flesh of deceased relatives. In doing so, they sometimes contracted kuru, a lethal neurological disease caused by a slow virus communicated by this cannibalism.[8]

In searching for societies that gave women favored status, one might expect that social systems that allowed women to have more than one husband at the same time would rank women as high as men if not higher. In fact, this is not the case. Polyandry, a form of marriage in which a woman is married to more than one man, has been practiced in Tibet, Nepal, India, Sri Lanka, and a few other places. Often, the multiple husbands are brothers. So it was among the Nyinba of Nepal, where fraternal polyandry was the approved form of marriage. Nevertheless, according to Nancy Levine, women were not regarded as men's equals. They were both politically and economically dependent on men, male kinship relationships were seen as more important, and there was a "lower valuation of women in general" along with a "greater concern and love for boys."[9]

Pastoral nomadic societies have typically displayed male dominance even more strongly than horticultural societies do, but there can be chivalry and romantic love at the same time. And even among pastoralists, women can sometimes achieve equality or something very close to it. As mentioned earlier, it was achieved among the Cheyenne of Wyoming. Although some writers have described ways in which men dominated women among the Cheyenne,[10] George Bird Grinnell, who lived among them at the turn of the century, strongly disagreed. He insisted that Cheyenne women "wielded an influence quite as important as [her husband's], and often even more powerful."[11]

> Among the Cheyennes, the women are the rulers of the camp. They act as a spur to the men, if they are slow in performing their duties. They are far more conservative than the men, and often hold them back from hasty, ill-advised action. If the sentiment of the women of the camp clearly points to a certain course as desirable, the men are quite sure to act as the women wish.[12]

Grinnell added that women

> discuss matters freely with their husbands, argue over points, persuade, cajole, and usually have their own way about tribal matters. They are, in fact, the final authority in the camp.[13]

Cheyenne women might sometimes fight if attacked, but despite their political authority, they were not warriors. However, among the Apaches, Seminoles, Creek, Shawnee, and Cherokee, women often went to war, although they had less political power than Cheyenne women.

In a seeming paradox, in more complex state societies with urban centers, the status of women tends to decline, although many women achieved great political power in Africa, particularly West Africa, and in these societies, women sometimes did go to war.[14] And as happened with the Dahomeans, when Western colonial powers came to govern non-Western peoples, the status of indigenous women has almost always declined, and their military activities have ended. In general, then, the record clearly indicates that when women are greatly unequal to man, they do not become warriors. But relatively high social status does not necessarily predict women's participation in warfare.

Most scholars familiar with the cross-cultural record would probably agree with this very general and brief summary of gender hierarchy without too many objections. But when it comes to explaining why these patterns have existed, agreement would quickly vanish. Some scholars would emphasize men's greater aggressiveness and physical strength, arguing that only under special circumstances could women overcome their relative physical weakness sufficiently to achieve parity. That women can be stronger than men, as was the case in Dahomey, has seldom been acknowledged.

Many contemporary women scholars appear to find nothing surprising about women's ability to perform well in roles previously reserved for men, believing that only male obstruction has prevented women from excelling in these ways in the past. But the conventional wisdom in anthropology—the scholarly discipline that most closely examines gender roles in all societies—has been more skeptical about women's ability to fill all traditionally "male" roles. For one thing, as Karen Brodkin Sacks has pointed out in her book *Sisters and Wives*, some of the leading scholars of the past have been ardent male chauvinists who have repeatedly denigrated women.[15] That kind of open chauvinism has lessened over time, but the conventional wisdom still dispensed in most anthropology textbooks today runs something like this: Because women alone could give birth, nurse infants, and provide infant care, and because their value for a small society in terms of future reproduction was far greater than that of men, throughout our evolution in small hunting and gathering societies, women tended to remain close to the safety of the camp, where they prepared food, cared for children, gathered nearby vegetable foods, and, some would unnecessarily add, gossiped. Meanwhile, men—bigger, stronger, and faster afoot—hunted game and raided neighbors. As a result, they claimed a monopoly over the manufacture and control of weapons, which were kept out of women's hands. It is inferred that over time this division of labor fostered male aggression and dominance, whereas women's potential for martial ardor diminished and their acceptance of male political and economic domination grew.[16]

So entrenched is this version of our ancestors that many anthropologists, or at least those who write introductory textbooks, appear to endorse the conclusion of Marvin Harris, and other distinguished anthropologists, that men have always been politically and economically dominant over women.[17] Many others have explained this dominance as a product of early human evolution that favored sexual dimorphism, male aggression and female submission.[18] Thus, some have referred to chimpanzees as models of our early ancestors. Because male chimps *(Pan troglodytes)* are larger and stronger than females and are often violent toward them, females became submissive to males. Also male chimps often kill not only infant chimps thought not to be their own offspring, but their neighbors as well. Murder and warfare occur, and they are male monopolies. Because we share over 98.5 percent of our DNA with chimpanzees, this model of our ancestry has had considerable power over our understanding of human evolution. "Chimpanzee" male dominance is not unlike that of many male humans over the known course of our history.[19]

Since the late 1970s, however, this model of the origins of male aggression and female submission has lost some of its appeal. For one thing, the discovery that another chimpanzee with whom we also share over 98.5 percent of our DNA, the so-called bonobo (*Pan paniscus,* or "pygmy chimp"), behaves in radically different ways, yet shares as many genes with us as its slightly larger relative, has led some to have second thoughts. Among bonobos, not only are males far less violent, but females actually dominate them—when necessary, by the use of force by several females against an offending male, but more often, it seems, by the use of food sharing and a truly remarkable devotion to what might be called "free love," that is, almost continuous sexual activity of virtually every sort practiced by humans.[20] Although a similar use of sex by females to pacify male aggression and to solidify ties between women and their sexual partners became part of the human portfolio, female dominance—if it actually exists among bonobos—did not.

Evolutionary psychology is a thriving new discipline, and among its most enduring interests are the psychobiological differences between men and women—differences in aggressivity, risk taking, nurturing, bonding, problem solving, and so on. In recent years, the field has made many advances, some of them based on the observation of primates, some on functional MRI studies of brain functions, others on the role of hormones in the development of gender.[21] However, this field has been hampered at times by a reliance on potentially culture-bound studies of child development or even more biased forms of psychological testing that often disadvantage women. Thus, although it is increasingly probable that women have greater language skills than men and that they have better spatial memory and olfactory acuity, other attributes, such as aggression, may be influenced by culture more than they are by nature. For example, it has long been a tenet of our cultural belief system that girls are less good at mathematics than boys. In fact, girls regularly outperform boys in tests of mathematics until their early teens, and although boys then tend to outperform girls at some forms of mathematics—for example, geometry—male and female test scores completely overlap.[22] It is also clear that there are subtle cultural factors that work against girls' success in mathematics. There may well prove to be cognitive skills that favor boys over girls in mathematics, spatial perception, and other cognitive or behavioral attributes, but this cannot be assumed until cultural beliefs about male and female abilities can be more fully examined and controlled for.[23] The desire and ability of women to engage in warfare may or may not be such a culture-bound attribute, but the power of culture to create inversions of gender roles has been powerfully documented in many parts of the world, for example, in early modern France by Natalie Zemon Davis.[24]

Other scholars give less weight to genetic inheritance and more to the value of women's economic contributions as the deciding factors in raising or lowering their status and increasing their involvement in war. But Iroquois women, as we have seen, had great economic power but no involvement in warfare. Still others would argue that, at least in small-scale societies, it is men's participation in warfare that matters most because, in general, the more that men engage in war, the lower women's status falls.[25] And there are many who would insist that no single factor predicts women's status or their involvement in warfare. They would see gender hierarchy as a product of multiple factors interacting in a complex historical context.

Several scholars have contended that matrilineal descent and matrilocal residence integrate men and women into more nearly coequal statuses because such systems disperse men throughout the society, integrating them into female kinship structures while separating them from male groups. Patrilineality, on the other hand, consolidates men into male-headed groups, encouraging male solidarity and dominance over women. Both assertions have value, but there are exceptions. As mentioned in Chapter 1, Peggy Reeves Sanday has offered yet another explanation for male dominance. After her review of the literature, she concluded that women tend to react to male dominance by conciliation, allowing men to hold sway in public venues while exercising control informally. But she added:

In other instances women fight for their rights. They succeed unless men kill a few token women to show that the battle for male domination is real. In these cases women acquiesce. They do not believe that "the trees that bear fruit" or "the mothers of men" should die.[26]

Sanday can be supported by a number of examples in which women in various societies have capitulated to men rather than risk their lives. However, in all but a handful of societies, men and women have achieved sufficient equilibrium in their dominance relationships that life-threatening challenges are rare. As a result, women almost everywhere have found ways of coping with husbands without putting their lives on the line. Among many ways of coping, some subtle, others not, they may resort to gossip, witchcraft, or subtle threats of poisoning their husbands. They may even take punitive collective actions in some societies where they are permitted to heap public ridicule, vituperation, and even physical abuse on a man who has flagrantly misbehaved.

In some small-scale societies, women suffered through life as painfully as Tasmanian women did, but in other societies, they struck back—hard. In Micronesia and several African societies, including the Pokot of Northern Kenya, women were entitled to come together in groups to punish an errant husband. For example, a Pokot wife who had been beaten too severely or had been deprived of sexual relations—and hence of children—by her husband could mobilize neighboring women to seize him while he slept, tie him to a tree (its bark studded with thorns), and beat him, his testicles sometimes included, soundly with sticks. While the women beat and reviled him, some might even urinate or defecate on him. When the women finally threatened to beat the husband to death, his wife intervened, pleading with them to spare him and promising that he would reform. He was then forced to agree to allow the women to slaughter an ox for them to feast upon, and not any ox but his favorite one, the one he painted decorations on and sang songs about. As they roasted the ox, the man wept.[27] Shirley Ardener has described similar practices elsewhere in Africa that were often called "sitting on a man."[28]

Women have also been known to take risky collective action against what they perceived to be political oppression. A famous example took place in 1929 among the Southern Igbo of Nigeria. Before British conquest, women's political and economic power among these people very nearly equaled that of men; each village had a women's council that had judicial powers over women, including the right to carry out capital punishment. Men were said to be quite nervous when the council met, fearing that women might also take action against them. In 1929, when women felt that a British colonial government edict would inflict economic hardship on them, they banded together from all over Igbo-land, attacking chiefs appointed by the British, then sacking European stores in a trading center. They were not stopped until British-led troops fired on them, killing fifty and wounding a similar number. Some Igbo men gave verbal support to the women, but they took no active part in the protest. This was not an isolated event. Among the Kom of Cameroon, women also took up arms to defend their rights, as they did in other parts of the world.[29]

And sometimes women have gone beyond these tactics to defend their rights. On the small island of Margarita off the coast of Venezuela, "Women are more violent than men in the expression of aggression."[30] Women not only fight with one another, often using their fists, but also attack men. For example, women were seen to tear the clothes off a policeman in a dispute over water. In general, male misconduct, such as rowdy drunkenness or disrespectful behavior, provokes female aggression: "If a man bothers me, I slap him in the face or I hit him over the head with a bottle. Once my women friends and I threw a guy on the ground because he was being disrespectful."[31] Women respect men's greater strength; one woman said that her husband was

"as strong as a dinosaur. But if he ever did anything to me, if he ever laid a hand on me, I could defend myself because he has to go to sleep sometime. If he ever disrespected me, I would wait until he slept and throw boiling oil on him."[32]

Because men on Margarita Island were often away fishing or working on the Venezuelan mainland, women became economically independent and socially dominant. They did not hesitate to risk harm by attacking men for misconduct, and men acquiesced in this aggression.

One of the most militant leaders of the Oyo, for many years Dahomey's overlords, was a woman, and as noted in Chapter 1, Igbo women of eastern Nigeria achieved a reputation for militancy when they rioted against British rule in 1929.[33] This was not an isolated example of their willingness to take risky collective action to rectify what they saw as wrongs; Igbo women often asserted their rights versus those of men. Igbo women belonged to village-based councils that dealt with all matters concerning women, including policing the markets and wards. The council met in private, surrounded by great secrecy. Men were said to be uneasy when a woman's council met because the council had the right to order mass strikes and demonstrations by all women. According to Igbo sociologist Ifi Amadiume:

> When ordered to strike, women refused to perform their expected duties and roles, including all domestic, sexual and maternal services. They would leave the town *en masse*, carrying only suckling babies. If angry enough, they were known to attack any men they met. Nothing short of the fulfillment of their demands would bring them back; but, by all indications, their demands were never unreasonable. They attacked viciously any decision or law which denied them, or interfered with, their means of livelihood, or the means by which they supported their children. Inter-town or inter-village wars might, for example, necessitate a temporary closure of some or all markets, or might render all market routes unsafe. Sexual harassment of young girls by young men might also make bush paths to markets unsafe. Disrespect by the men, such as making laws binding to women, or deciding levies for the whole town without the knowledge and consent of the women, were all matters dealt with by the Woman's Council.[34]

Great power, indeed, but well short of female dominance. Igbo women possessed marked respect and power. Their culture allowed them to assert their rights without assuming male gender roles, and some powerful and assertive women dominated their husbands without being criticized by others. Women could gain power within their lineage, too, but in general, men nevertheless had more power than women in public activities, women could not own land, and women felt some unease when filling positions normally held by men.[35] Still, for the most part, a balance of respect between men and women existed that was matched in very few societies. Despite their political power and their willingness to act aggressively, neither the Igbo women nor the women of Margarita Island engaged in warfare.

Sometimes, women have earned men's respect and gained political power without any display of militancy. So it was among the Lovedu, a cattle-herding people of southern Africa. The Lovedu were patrilineal, reckoning descent in the male line, and patrilocal as well, wives moving into the villages of their husbands. Cattle herding, the source of Lovedu wealth and livelihood, was also exclusively a male activity. Yet, for some 200 years, the Lovedu were ruled by queens. District heads were often, but not always, male, but they were clearly under the authority of the queen. The source of the queen's power was not her bravery or combativeness but, instead, the supernatural ability to make rain that a queen was thought to possess—and was required to demonstrate when drought threatened.[36]

In societies around the world, women have also avoided death in warfare, doing everything they can to protect their own lives and those of their children while encouraging their men to deal with the enemy. But this was not the case everywhere, as the Amazons of Dahomey so dramatically demonstrated. In searching for an explanation for the central role given to women in Dahomey's armies, we must first acknowledge that most small-scale societies around the world have not used women as warriors. In some of these societies, men actively forbade women to take up arms in military combat, and in others, women wanted no part of warfare. For example, until defeated by British troops in 1879, Zulu warriors were the scourge of southern Africa, their spear-stabbing soldiers seemingly invincible. Zulu women exercised considerable influence, running their households as they saw fit, holding prestigious positions as diviners and priestesses, and wielding substantial political power. Princess Mkhabayi virtually ruled the kingdom after the death of King Shaka. The succeeding kings were her nephews, and they were terrified of her.[37] Young Zulu women urged men on to war and could even prevent a newly mobilized regiment from going to war by stripping themselves naked and standing in the soldiers' path. But they did not become soldiers themselves. They did not even carry supplies for the Zulu warriors when they went to war.

In West Africa, where warfare was endemic during the nineteenth century, one of the largest and most formidable armies in that area fought for the Kingdom of Asante in what is now Ghana. The Asante fought against British troops in several major battles throughout the century, and despite a great inferiority in weapons, they sometimes won. They were not finally conquered until 1900, when they again fought bravely but this time faced machine guns and modern artillery firing high-explosive shells. The wives of an Asante commander might sometimes follow him to battle, and some wives accompanied their soldier husbands to cook for them. Asante women also supported war by urging men on to battle and shaming anyone who shirked his duty. But unlike Dahomean women, they did not fight in combat.[38]

The picturesque highlands of Papua New Guinea, especially the eastern portion of this large territory, were the scene of almost continuous warfare between the small societies of farmers and pig raisers who lived there, but seldom in peace. While the men shouted insults at their enemies, then showered them with arrows, women and children watched from a safe distance, typically taking no part in the conflict and, in fact, usually enjoying immunity from harm. The Kapauku, for example, considered it immoral to fire an arrow at a woman. According to Pospisil:

When I saw for the first time a Kapauku battle I could hardly believe my eyes. While the men were engaged in deadly combat, and dead and wounded warriors were being carried away, many of the women, obviously undisturbed, were quietly collecting arrows on, behind, and between the battle lines, as if they were harvesting potatoes or cucumbers. Several of the bolder members of the "weaker" sex even climbed a hill behind the enemy's lines and, from there, shouted advice concerning the enemy's movements to their fighting husbands. The annoyed and embarrassed enemy could only try to chase the women away by pushing them or beating them with bows and fists. Aside from the mortification of having to contend with the women, the warriors were often not even assured of success in routing them because the women wielded walking sticks, usually much longer than a bow, and it was sometimes the men who received the pushing and beating.[39]

Unlike these audacious but invulnerable Kapauku women, most women in this violent region hated war. They feared the loss of their husbands or sons, especially the rigors of widowhood that could force them to support themselves with little assistance. Mae Enga women tried to talk their men out of it when they saw them preparing for battle, but without success: "'Although we tend the gardens and feed the children and pigs, we are only women, and the men never listen to us.'" Men agreed, "'Yes,' they said, 'women generally do not like their menfolk to go to war, but we take no notice of their fears. These matters do not concern them; they must do as they are told.'"[40]

The six member nations that made up the Iroquois Confederacy gave women such extraordinary powers that some scholars in the past proposed them as the world's only matriarchy. This was an exaggeration, but women in these six societies did have exceptional prestige and power.[41] Girl babies were cherished; women ruled everything about the family and controlled almost everything in the economy. Women appointed the chiefs, who were male, and could remove them, if need be. They also lived in a society that reckoned descent and inheritance in the female line. Men were warriors, often away on long campaigns, and this was their domain. An occasional woman, especially among the Seneca, went to war with the men, and an occasional woman warrior won high honors for her bravery, but these were exceptions. The great majority of Iroquois women did nothing to translate their economic and political power into equality on the battlefield. They were not warriors, and men felt superior to women despite all else.[42]

Throughout precolonial North and South America, warfare was frequent, savage, and almost universal. Everywhere on the continent, war was the province primarily of men. Trained to become hardy and brave as children, males usually accompanied warriors on raids while still adolescents and soon after became accomplished fighters. Many raids were relatively bloodless, their goal being the taking of valuables or the capture of women, but sometimes the goal was extermination of the enemy, leaving many hundreds dead and no prisoners taken.[43] Some women occasionally went to war in a number of New World societies, and in a few, like the Inca, they played a prominent role, using slingshots to throw missiles at their enemies, including Spanish conquistadores. Nevertheless, no society in the Americas appears to have systematically trained women to become warriors, much less the elite corps of a standing army as happened in Dahomey. In fact, in all but a handful of New World tribal societies, women were not only never trained for war but were also actively excluded from anything involving combat, usually with the expressed belief that their presence during warfare would result in catastrophe. Unlike the Amazons of Dahomey, these women were taught to look upon war as the exclusive domain of men.

Despite this strong cultural pressure to exclude women from warlike activities, in some New World societies women went to war anyway, sometimes going into battle alongside men and earning honors for their bravery. Even in societies where women had far fewer rights than they did among the Iroquois, a few women took on male roles, dressed as men, married women, and went to war. Sometimes, they were such skillful and brave warriors that they earned honors. Among North American Plains Indians, a

Crow woman who scalped an enemy received songs of praise,[44] and women in neighboring societies were known to so distinguish themselves in battle that they were made chiefs and allowed to marry several wives.[45]

Among the Ojibwa, who lived to the east and north of the Great Lakes, this pattern was particularly common. Although women were discouraged from hunting or going on raids with men, they sometimes did so nevertheless to revenge someone's death or simply for "excitement and glory."[46] Some of these women went to war, won honors, counted coup, danced like men, and behaved as arrogantly as men. They could be awarded the honor of wearing eagle feathers and given the title of "brave." Other women looked at them askance, but in general, "The people are untroubled by the contradiction between a woman's earning this title and the conventional belief that war is a male occupation closed to women and inimically affected by their proximity."[47] In recognition of the fact that some women in many New World Indian societies chose to behave and dress like men, a number of societies developed a transgendered role for them. Among the Piegan of the Northern Plains, it was known as "the manly-hearted woman," although the Piegan women who adopted this role seldom actually engaged in warfare.[48] Like the Amazons of Dahomey, these women who chose to go to war "became" men.

The women soldiers of Dahomey were not an isolated instance of female bravery in combat in Africa. Regiments made up exclusively of women were known in many parts of Africa from the Sudan to Zimbabwe, and in much of West Africa and Angola. A member of Vasco de Gama's expedition along the coast of West Africa reported seeing legions of perhaps 6,000 women soldiers in West Africa some 300 years before the Amazons of Dahomey came into being.[49] And led by the redoubtable Queen Zhinga Mbande Ngola, women of the Kingdom of Ngola in Angola fought well against the Portuguese. Queen Zhinga impressed with her military ability a Dutch officer who was there to help her people expel the Portuguese. He was also impressed by the use Queen Zhinga made of a harem made up of some sixty handsome young men. In more recent times, women played a large role in the deadly combat that was known as the Mau Mau rebellion in Kenya, and just before World War I, Herero women in Namibia fought bravely against Imperial German troops. After Malawi received its independence, its leader, Dr. Hastings Banda, used an all-woman army to police the border with neighboring Tanzania. In the recent combat between Ethiopia and Eritrea, many of Eritrea's most stalwart troops were women.

In South America, the tribal society that gave the greatest freedom to women was probably the Abipone, horse nomads of the Gran Chaco in Paraguay. Before they were finally decimated by Spanish forces, the Abipone gave great political power to women, who often served as chiefs and influential shamans. Abipone women were aggressive and competitive, often fighting with one another and even hitting men. On festive occasions, they held violent wrestling matches while men looked on. But although the Abipone were almost continually at war with neighboring tribes and Spanish settlers, their women did not participate in warfare.[50]

Women in small-scale societies now and then went to war for revenge or glory, but among the Celts, they often did so, earning a reputation for ferocity. As towns and cities grew around the world, women often fought to defend them against invaders, and women have now and then joined armies throughout history, usually disguised as men and serving in the ranks, even sometimes as leaders. Many did so during the American Civil War and various European wars. One British army private who was a woman disguised as a man served for sixteen years before being killed at Waterloo.[51] Women have occasionally become military commanders in all parts of the world, and sometimes women have played a major role in combat. This was true in most of Asia, the Middle East, and Africa. In Siam, some 400 women served as elite royal guards but, despite being trained for combat, did not go to war. And women in many parts of India not only sometimes led male troops but also sometimes served in all-female units during World War II.[52] During this same war, 25,000 Yugoslavian women were killed fighting the Germans as partisans, and 40,000 were wounded. Another 282,000 partisan women died in concentration camps.[53]

A few Russian women became heroines during the War of 1812, and although Russian women did not take up weapons during the Crimean War of 1854–1856, they did exhibit exceptional bravery under fire while the port city of Sevastopol was bombarded for nearly a year. During World War I, some Russian women served in all-female combat units, and when the revolution of 1917–1918 came, women soldiers tried to defend the Winter Palace, while Bolshevik women joined men in storming it. Russian women's most remarkable military achievements came in World War II.

Facing a German onslaught that occupied a third of the country and killed a tenth of the Soviet population before the war ended, almost a million Soviet women volunteered to fight. Over 127,000 women served as partisans in the forests, often engaging in hand-to-hand fighting, and always experiencing great danger and hardship. While many women served in support roles as nurses, radio or telephone operators, supply truck drivers, and other noncombat positions, some 500,000 women saw action at the front in nearly every capacity imaginable.[54] They drove tanks, fought as armed medical aides, flew ancient biplane night bombers and modern fighter planes, commanded gun detachments, and served as snipers in the ruins of Stalingrad, where one woman was credited with killing 309 Germans.[55] Many were awarded medals for valor. Many others were killed or maimed. When the war ended, women no longer were trained for combat roles. Those women who fought in World War II and survived were neither surprised nor regretful about this change in policy, saying that the physical demands of prolonged combat were too terrible for women.[56]

Just as Soviet women volunteered to fight for their country in 1941, Israeli women fought in Israel's War of Independence in 1947–1949. As early as the 1920s, Israel's underground army, the Haganah, trained women in armed defense. Many women belonged to Jewish underground forces that employed terrorist tactics against the British, killing many British soldiers. After World War II ended, Israeli women continued their terrorist activities focused on stealing guns or smuggling them into the country. Others joined the Palmach, an elite underground military force that subjected women to the same rigorous physical activity and use of weapons as men. As one woman recalled:

> We had to run three kilometers each morning in hiking shoes with knapsacks on our backs. We had to know how to run long distances in the field. We also learned judo, first aid and weaponry. We learned to shoot and throw grenades. We even learned to fight with sticks, because it was illegal for us to possess weapons under the British Mandate.[57]

When fighting broke out against Palestinians after the British forces withdrew, women fought alongside men in gender-mixed combat units. Israel's army eventually numbered 60,000, 12,000 of whom were women. Most women performed admirably and were well accepted by male soldiers, but under pressure from a number of sources, especially Orthodox Jews, the army finally agreed to place women in their own units and to remove them from combat situations. Women still serve in the Israeli armed forces and are trained in the use of weapons, but they have not been used in combat since the War for Independence ended. Abba Eban's autobiography makes no mention of women's contribution to that war, and neither does David Ben Gurion's.[58]

Women not only have been willing to face violent death in wars for national survival but have also done so for political causes in countries as diverse as Algeria, Cuba, Mozambique, and Vietnam. Large numbers of women also fought in El Salvador. In many parts of the world in recent years, women who were oppressed under patriarchal governmental structures and cultural values joined with men to bring about revolutionary change. They did so with great courage, often risking their lives, and they sometimes helped to bring about changes that benefited most people as well as political and property rights that particularly benefited women. So it was in China, Bolivia, Indonesia, and Mexico, among other countries. But even in these societies, gender inequality was seldom transformed and never eliminated, as male dominance endured in places as diverse as Angola, Afghanistan, Chile, Iran, Israel, Mozambique, and Yugoslavia.[59] An example comes from Kenya in the early 1950s, when many thousands of men and women attempted to bring an end to British rule. Most of the people who fought in this movement were Kikuyu, an ethnic group that was clearly dominated by men. Women did almost all of the hard labor and were forced to undergo clitoral excision and to marry older men whom they often did not favor in return for a payment of valuables to their father.

Despite often oppressive male dominance, and despite the fact that there was no tradition of women going to war among the Kikuyu, thousands of Kikuyu women joined men in war camps in the vast mountainous forest of central Kenya. Because the rebels had so few weapons, women were sent out of the forest camps to buy or steal weapons and ammunition, a risky activity that was closely watched by British soldiers, Kenya police, and large numbers of armed African home guardsmen. Some women smuggled ammunition back to the forest concealed in their vaginas. Many women received military training and fought in deadly battles against the British and Kikuyu loyalists, for whom other Kikuyu women also fought. One major Mau Mau unit was led by a woman, and other women achieved high military rank. When Mau Mau women were captured, they were often interrogated barbarically; their heads were held under water, and they were then choked and burned with cigarettes. Poisonous snakes were inserted into their vaginas, where it was also common for their torturers to pour boiling water. After the rebellion was finally defeated, a Mau Mau leader declared that Mau Mau women were braver than men.[60] Following the rebellion, some Kikuyu women achieved greater gender equality, but the force of male dominance was not ended. Men continued to control the Kikuyu economy and politics.

Women took part in the war effort by North Vietnam against the French—and later the Americans—in large numbers. They fought in all-female guerrilla units, often achieving remarkable success.

They also served in antiaircraft units, engaged in espionage, and carried tons of supplies to fighting units. Yet, as the war went on, women were slowly phased out of frontline combat roles. This appears to have taken place because increasing numbers of male soldiers had doubts about women's physical and temperamental ability to perform extended combat roles.[61] Nonetheless, so many women fought that the North Vietnamese army was known as the "long-haired army," and casualties among women were extensive. In the south alone, from 1954 to 1965, 250,000 women were killed, 40,000 were disabled by torture, and another 36,000 died in prison.[62]

Paradoxically, the People's Republic of China, whose ideology inspired the government of North Vietnam, did not give women a prominent role in combat. Although some 3,000 women accompanied men on the "Long March" and some joined them in guerrilla warfare, as the People's Liberation Army became more organized women were restricted to noncombat roles. This began in 1937, during the war against Japan, and has continued since that time. Women in China were granted many political and economic rights that had not been theirs before, but they were not allowed near battle.[63] All-women battalions fought bravely during the Tai Ping peasant revolt of 1850–1864, and many heroines are known throughout Chinese history, but women typically went to war only during severe crises or to replace a key male family member who was unable to carry out his military duties. In modern times, the Chinese restriction of women from combat was influenced by the Soviet Union's postwar policy against the continued use of women in combat.[64] Nevertheless, large numbers of women have served in noncombat roles, thirteen of them advancing to the rank of general by 1994.[65]

In the United States, Canada, and the NATO countries since World War II, women have slowly increased in numbers in those countries' armed forces. Today, women make up almost 11 percent of Canada's armed forces, and over 200,000 women serve in the U.S. military. In recent years, growing numbers of women have been trained for combat roles. Danish women command tanks, and

Norway has a woman commander of a submarine.[66] Although American women are not permitted to serve in U.S. submarines, five women command surface combat ships. And although the U.S. Army and Marines still proscribe combat duty in the infantry, armor, field artillery, or special forces, in 1993 the U.S. Department of Defense opened combat aviation to women.[67] American women have also come under hostile fire. One hundred and fifty women were in combat during the Panamanian action of 1990, and forty-one thousand women served in Operation Desert Storm. Five of these were killed by hostile fire, and two were captured. One of these, Captain Rhonda Cornum, a doctor, was raped both vaginally and rectally even though both her arms were badly broken when her helicopter was shot down.[68] She survived to write about her ordeal but did not admit to her rape until after her book was published, perhaps because the fear that women prisoners would be raped has often been put forward as a reason to keep women out of combat. In late 1998, sixteen American women flew combat missions over Iraq during Operation Desert Fox.

Seen against this background, it would be possible to argue that women have engaged in armed combat in so many parts of the world for so long that the emergence of an elite force of female troops in Dahomey is hardly a surprise. In one sense, that is true. Women around the world have proven themselves capable of excelling as warriors. It is also possible that somewhere on earth, perhaps in West Africa as some observers have suggested, women have served as the elite battalions of other armies. But the evidence for these suggestions is scanty at best. Nowhere beyond Dahomey do we have detailed knowledge of an army that was led by female troops for any length of time.

If the Amazons of Dahomey are unique or nearly so, how can we explain their emergence and long tenure as the shock troops of a kingdom whose army was both successful and greatly feared by its enemies? We can begin by repeating the plausible explanation that because Dahomean kings did not permit men to enter their palaces after nightfall, their guards, at least at night, had to be women. Being large, powerful, and swift women trained to use all available weapons, when the chance came for them to use their weapons in combat they no doubt used them well, as women have proven able to do in many parts of the world. That chance may have come early in the eighteenth century, when Dahomey's army of male troops was badly depleted by war against the Oyo. Later, after being chosen to serve as elite troops by King Gezo sometime after 1818, and given the honors, privileges, and intense training that set them apart from and above male soldiers, it is likely that they developed their military fervor and skills even further. It is clear that male and female soldiers competed with each other, spurring the other gender on in exhibitions of bravery and military skill. A system like this, once in place, was likely to endure. Despite the defeats at Abeokuta, it took near annihilation at the hands of the French to end this one.

This line of argument has a certain plausibility, but a nagging question remains: If Dahomey's women warriors were such loyal and successful soldiers, why didn't other West African kingdoms, which were sometimes all too familiar with Dahomey's Amazons, create female armies of their own? Neither the Asante nor the Yoruba kingdoms such as the Oyo and the Egba used women as warriors, even though all these peoples fought against Dahomey. Indeed, Yoruba women usually actively opposed war.[69] Smaller kingdoms in the area, many of which were ultimately destroyed by Dahomey, did not use women warriors either, although some, including Whydah, used women as palace guards. These societies permitted some women to help men during battle, usually by bringing them food, but women did not fight. It would be one thing if Dahomey were a weak state, forced to use women as a last, desperate measure, but this was not the case at any point during the 200 years that Amazons were known to exist in Dahomey. It has sometimes been argued that Dahomean women achieved their elite military status only because so many Dahomean men had been killed during incessant warfare—or shipped overseas as slaves—that women had to be pressed into service. Male losses in warfare may well have been heavy, but men always made up the great majority of Dahomey's professional soldiers, usually outnumbering women by three or four to one. Dahomean women were the elite of their kingdom's army, but never its majority.

It is true that both the Asante and the Yoruba had far more populous kingdoms than Dahomey, and it might be argued that Dahomey's use of women as soldiers was an attempt to even the odds. But Dahomey fought against the Asante only once, late in the eighteenth century, and the Yoruba-speaking peoples were divided among a dozen or more separate kingdoms. Dahomey's main Yoruba opponents during the nineteenth century, the Egba, were not notably more numerous, pitting some 15,000 soldiers against perhaps 12,000 Dahomean troops. What may be even more significant, the Yoruba-speaking Oyo domination of the early eighteenth century took place at a time when Dahomey could have used a large force of well-trained women warriors to even the odds somewhat against the more numerous Oyo, but there were apparently never more than 1,000 or so Amazons under arms at any time during the Oyo wars.

The best explanation for the emergence of women as Dahomey's military elite lies elsewhere than the need for larger numbers of troops. First, West African monarchs greatly feared palace coups, and all sought protection against them. Some emphasized religious protection of various sorts, whereas others relied on political alliances, but in addition to these precautions, some surrounded themselves with palace guards who would have loyalty to the king alone and would defend him against any opponents. The Asante, for example, used foreign soldiers, especially men from the warlike Hausa, as palace guards, and several West African kingdoms used women in this role. As we have seen, Dahomean women proved to be exceptionally loyal palace guards. After King Gezo took power, he chose to expand the ranks of his women soldiers, honoring them not only as his loyal guards but as the premier troops of his marauding army.

With Gezo's encouragement, Amazon officers took over, creating superior means of military training as well as the inculcation of values and attitudes that led to a vibrant esprit de corps involving overt competition with male soldiers, boasts of becoming men, and actual leadership in battle. By 1850, male and female soldiers openly quarreled, insulting each other during legislative sessions and no doubt at other times as well. For Dahomey, the combination of honors, tangible rewards such as cowries or slaves, rigorous training, and fierce competition succeeded so well in creating a devoted and skilled body of women warriors it is surprising that no other West African society chose to emulate Dahomey. Many armies now and in times past have proven that men can develop remarkable morale when treated as elite warriors. Dahomey proved that women can achieve that same thing.

Dahomey's Amazons, many of them captives from other societies, proved themselves to be immensely loyal, brave, skillful, even ferocious warriors. All who saw them in action declared them better soldiers than Dahomey's male warriors. France's elite Foreign Legionnaires and Marine Infantry admitted that they had all they could do to defeat the Amazons despite the great advantage that artillery, machine guns, and bayonets gave them. That no other society chose to develop elite women warriors as Dahomey did may speak volumes about men's attitudes toward women, but it says nothing about women's limitations as warriors.

The Amazons and Women in Military Combat Today

With the end of the draft in the United States in 1973, an all-volunteer military force came into being, and with it came increasing numbers of women in all branches of military service. Following the passage of P.L. 94-106, U.S. military academies were opened to women in 1980, women officers being commissioned four years later. From this time on, more and more women, including many from ethnic and racial minorities, enlisted in the armed forces, hoping for vocational training and anticipating the rewards due them at the time of honorable discharge, such as "GI bill" financing of a college education.[70] Today, roughly 12 percent of the personnel in America's military are female. Although Israel was the only country to draft women,

women also enlisted in many Western military forces during the same period, Italy being the only NATO country to exclude women from its armed forces.[71]

This entry of sizable numbers of women into Western armed forces led to an explosion of male indignation about the "feminization" of the military, something that continues to this day.[72] Although women in several countries have been authorized to fly combat aircraft, and to command warships, submarines, and tanks, they have not yet achieved significant roles in combat infantry units or field artillery. Men continue to complain, sometimes stridently, that the presence of women in their military units has a demoralizing effect on them, just as they argue that many combat roles require greater physical strength and emotional endurance than all but a few women possess. There are men in the armed forces of various countries who support the use of women in combat roles, just as there are women in the military who have no desire to engage in combat.[73] But the controversy continues, and it is for this reason that the experiences of the Amazons of Dahomey take on contemporary relevance.

One frequently voiced concern by military men has to do with women's lack of "natural" aggressiveness, making reference to many anecdotal instances in which women have been seen to be less aggressive than men. Some more scholarly military writers have cited the well-known, and often considered to be authoritative, study of psychologists Eleanor Maccoby and Carol Jacklin that found males to be more aggressive than females in all known societies, a difference said to result from gender differences in levels of testosterone.[74] More recent research has cast doubt on this sweeping assertion. Although Maccoby and Jacklin were correct in reporting that boys tend to engage in rough-and-tumble play more often than girls do, how aggressive the two genders become later in life varies considerably from one culture to another, so much so that it is now generally believed that culture is more predictive of aggression than gender.[75] To mention but one example, the American South has long been characterized by the crucial place of honor in people's lives. To protect their honor, southern men have long been quick to resort to violence, but so have southern women, committing homicide far more often than women anywhere else in the United States.[76]

It would not be surprising if many women who have recently enlisted in the armed forces of Western countries were less aggressive than their male counterparts because these countries typically socialize females to be less aggressive than males. But as the Amazons, among others, so dramatically demonstrated, women who take on the role of warrior during their adolescent years not only can become as aggressive as male soldiers but can also be even more ferocious than men in combat. What is more, the war against the French showed that even very young, recent conscripts would fight ferociously.

Another concern often expressed about women serving in modern armies is their relative lack of upper body strength. For this reason, it is often said and written that women in the infantry would be a liability because most of them could not carry their more-than-100-pound rucksacks for any great distance, nor could they carry a wounded comrade, especially a 200-pound man, to safety. However, recent research in the United Kingdom and the United States has shown that six months of training can develop sufficient strength in women for them to match men in the physical skills necessary for infantry service.[77] This finding, if correct, does not mean that women recruits can reasonably be expected to match physically gifted, highly trained men in elite "special forces" units such as U.S. Army Rangers or Navy SEALS. But in some societies, like Dahomey, women engaged in more strenuous physical activity than men, becoming more heavily muscled than men and capable of great physical exertion. Dahomey's Amazons were chosen from the largest and strongest of young women, usually in their early adolescence. Years of rigorous training, including hours of athletic dancing, long marches, wall climbing, and weapons handling, created a corps of mature women that was stronger, faster afoot, and capable of greater endurance than Dahomean male soldiers, who were typically less strong when they entered the army and then received less rigorous training.

Another frequently expressed concern involves menstruation and pregnancy. As recently as World War II, women on hazardous-duty field assignments reported that menstruation made their lives difficult. Soviet women serving in frontline units against the Germans complained about the embarrassment and debilitation they experienced during their menses, as did women in other armies.[78] In recent years, menstruation has seldom been mentioned as a problem by either women or men in Western armed forces. Pregnancy, however, remains an issue, one that many would say is the most central problem for women in the military.[79] It is not only that pregnant women soldiers would be limited in their combat duty effectiveness during at least the latter months of their pregnancy, but after giving birth they would also be unavailable for combat duty for some months and perhaps longer if adequate child-care services were not available. These concerns are self-evident, but of equal weight in the minds of many is the specter of young mothers dying in battle.[80]

As we have seen, the Dahomeans addressed the problem of pregnancy by imposing on their women soldiers an absolute prohibition against sexual intercourse with men, as well as the apparently mandatory consumption of contraceptive herbs. There is no information about menstrual problems that may have troubled the Amazons. With the availability of modern contraceptives, there need be no pregnancies among female soldiers today, but women who wish to serve in combat infantry units would presumably be required to agree to postpone motherhood for the period of their military service. If the past is any guide, women in the armed forces who were not in combat roles would continue to become pregnant with some frequency. Women who agree to postpone pregnancy to serve in combat roles would presumably have to be given incentives to do so.

As crucial as the question of pregnancy is for women in the military, concerns about male bonding and male pride may be even more basic. Men in the military often complain that the presence of women in their units weakens the male bonds they so cherish, converting them from "buddies" bonded together in common cause, into competitors for the admiration or sexual favors of women. Men also resent women's intrusion into the "masculine" world of the military, a place where generations of men have taken great pride in exhibiting manly virtues such as bravery, loyalty, and steadfastness. When women enter this world and exhibit the same qualities, men can feel diminished. Although men's hostility to women soldiers often focuses on their inability to perform adequately in special forces where male physical attributes far exceed those of women, male hostility is widespread throughout the military. That women in the military are so commonly thought of by men as "dykes" or "whores" has led most military women to go to some lengths to reduce either their femininity or their masculinity, sometimes choosing an asexual portrayal of themselves.[81] When women officers first served on U.S. Navy ships, men refused to accept them or their authority.[82] Some observers have likened men's rejection of women in their military units to the racial exclusion policies of earlier times.

Women never served alongside men in Dahomey's army. They were conscripted, housed, and trained apart from men throughout their years of service. And although they sometimes fought side by side with men, they were always in their own separate units, led by women officers. Competition between male and female units was openly encouraged, and both genders took to it with relish, probably increasing the combat effectiveness of both male and female units. Competition engendered hostility, too. Men were scornful when women insisted in their songs and chants that they had become men. Recall King Glele's dismissive aside to Richard Burton that "they are still women." They also quarreled in public, accusing one another of cowardice or ineptitude as warriors. But there is no record of armed conflict between male and female troops, and the evidence suggests that gender competition increased the effectiveness of both Dahomey's men and women soldiers.

A final concern is women's ability to withstand the stresses of prolonged combat. Although military commentators, often retired officers, acknowledge the courage and fighting skills of Soviet women during World War II, they also point to disclosures by some Soviet women who survived the war, that the physical and emotional demands of combat were so burdensome that they had no desire to serve in combat again, or to see their daughters do so in the future.[83] Similar concerns were noted in North Vietnam and other countries that employed women extensively in combat. And there is considerable discussion by contemporary military leaders about the ability of women to withstand the rigors of basic training or protracted exposure to difficult field conditions. The impressive success of most American service women in enduring the hazards and discomforts of service during the Gulf War has impressed some male military leaders, but by no means all are convinced that women belong in harm's way.[84]

In this regard, the Amazons may once again be instructive. They endured training that was more rigorous than that experienced by Dahomean men, ran through thornbush barricades until blood flowed down their legs with no hint of pain, and cheerfully outlasted men on long, hungry, and dangerous campaigns. Over a two-month period in 1892, they fought in thirty-two bloody battles against the French, maintaining their morale and enthusiasm for close combat to the very end. More formidable, steadfast soldiers would be difficult to imagine.

The model that the Amazons offer should be intriguing to today's military leaders. What made the Amazons into the phenomenally loyal, brave, and battle-ready troops that they became is simple enough to identify. First, whether they were slaves or free Dahomean women, Dahomey's kings reposed trust in them, gave them high honors and valuable rewards, and elevated them to the pinnacle of public admiration. For the most part, physically powerful young women were conscripted in their early adolescence, then trained under strict discipline to become hardy, pain-resistant, skilled fighters. Most who were not killed in battle served in this role for many years, two or more decades of continuous service not being uncommon. They lived in separate barracks, trained separately from men, and fought in all-female units, encouraged at all times to exceed the best efforts of male soldiers. Their successes were publicly recognized by gifts, honors, privileges, and popular acclaim.

There is nothing mysterious about the model used to create the Amazons as a premier fighting force. With the exception of pregnancy control, it is closely similar to the practices used by many countries to create elite male military units. The Dahomean experience suggests that if strong young women today were recruited young, were sworn to defer pregnancy, were trained long and hard in all-female units, were given prizes and privileges, were encouraged to compete with all-male units, and were honored for their loyalty, bravery, and battlefield success, there is no reason to believe that they would not become exemplary combat soldiers. Yet, as feminist scholars have argued and military leaders in many countries including the United States increasingly acknowledge, there are many combat roles that women can fill in admirable fashion without being subjected to the radical recruitment, training, and gender transformation undergone by the Amazons.[85]

Perhaps the last word about the women warriors of Dahomey should be this: The Amazons tell us a great deal about what women are capable of accomplishing as warriors, but they do not offer us guidance when it comes to deciding whether women in various contemporary societies ought to be used in military roles. That decision involves complex political, economic, religious, and cultural issues that each nation must address in its own terms. But as leaders of these nations do so, it might prove useful for them to reflect on the history and achievement of the women warriors of Dahomey.

Notes

Introduction

1. Keegan (1993: 76).

2. Van Creveld (1993: 5).

3. De Pauw (1998).

4. Jones (1997); De Pauw (1998).

5. Both Jones and De Pauw have provided brief accounts of the women soldiers of Dahomey, as have many other historians, but for extended descriptions readers should see d'Almeida-Topor (1984), for her account in French, and Alpern (1998), for a more extensive and detailed description in English.

6. Ghiglieri (1999: 184). For a comparable analysis of primate violence, see Wrangham and Peterson (1996). For a discussion of the "natural violence" of women, see Kirsta (1994).

7. Bay (1977).

8. Bay (1998).

9. M'Leod (1820: 129).

10. Cruickshank (1848: 187).

11. Rice (1900).

12. Burton (1864, Vol. 2). See also Cairns (1965: 85), Davidson (1967: 24).

13. Penzer (1924: 131).

14. Carlyle (1849: 677).

15. Reader (1998).

16. Isichei (1977: 112).

17. Edgerton (1995).

18. Kea (1971: 205).

19. d'Albéca (1895: 218); Kea (1971: 206).

20. Valdez (1861: 351).

21. M'Leod (1820: 36).

22. Fage (1992: 1).

23. Ibid.: 24.

24. Davidson and Buah (1965: 51–52).

25. Davis-Kimball (1997). See also De Pauw (1998).

26. Markale (1968: 172).

27. Kleinbaum (1983: 172).

28. How many of these Europeans were familiar with the so-called Amazons of past history is not always clear from their writings, but important visitors like Forbes (1851) and Burton (1864) often wrote about Dahomean Amazons.

Chapter 1

1. Bosman (1721: 231–232).

2. Manning (1982: 9).

3. Quoted in Burton (1864, Vol. 1: 13).

4. Ibid.: xv.

5. Ibid.: 165.

6. M'Leod (1820: 30); Burton (1864, Vol. 1: 96).

7. Norris (1789: 72).

8. Forbes (1851, Vol. 1: 59).

9. Ibid.: 65.

10. Wilmot, quoted in Burton (1864, Vol. 2: 372).

11. Burton (1864, Vol. 1: 281).

12. Herskovits (1938, Vol. 1: 4).

13. Guillevin (1862: 32).

14. Edgerton (1995).

15. Répin (1863: 99); Hazoumé (1938).

16. Bay (1998: 174).

17. Law (1993: 250).

18. Degbelo (1989).

19. d'Almeida-Topor (1984: 33–36).

20. Snelgrave (1734: 125–127).

21. Bay (1977: 164).

22. Snelgrave (1734: 77–79).
23. M'Leod (1820: 45–46).
24. Quoted in Burton (1864, Vol. 2: 346).
25. Ibid.: 340.
26. Ibid.: 345.
27. Ibid.:, 367.
28. Quoted in Alpern (1998: 115).
29. d'Almeida-Topor (1984: 64).
30. Burton (1864, Vol. 1: 169–170).
31. Skertchly (1874: 454–455).
32. Maroukis (1974: 90).
33. See Law (1993: 256), Degbelo (1989: 108–109), and Bay (1998: 206).
34. Alpern (1998: 99).
35. Burton (1864, Vol. 2: 68).
36. Degbelo (1989: 98).
37. Bay (1998: 145).
38. Répin (1863: 100).
39. Duncan (1847: 234).
40. Hazoumé (1925).
41. Herskovits (1938, Vol. 2: 87).
42. Bay (1983: 352).
43. Alpern (1998).
44. Duncan (1847: 225–230).
45. Forbes (1851, Vol. 2: 120).
46. Degbelo (1989: 168).
47. Skertchly (1874: 344).
48. Bayol (1892: 522).
49. Ajayi and Smith (1964: 52).
50. Forbes (1851, Vol. 1: 27).
51. Quénum (1981: 57).
52. Law (1993: 258).
53. Burton (1864, Vol. 1: 72).
54. Bay (1977: 21).
55. Forbes (1851, Vol. 2: 108).
56. Nardin (1967: 98).
57. Duncan (1847, Vol. 1: 227).

58. Burton (1864, Vol. 2: 79).
59. d'Almeida-Topor (1984:106).
60. Aublet (1894: 103); Chaudoin (1891: 186).
61. Martyn (1911: 233).
62. Degbelo (1989: 114).
63. Forbes (1851, Vol. 1: 78).
64. Duncan (1847, Vol. 1: 232).
65. Ibid.: 233.
66. Bay (1977: 176).
67. Conneau (1976: 204–205).
68. Burton (1864, Vol. 2: 376).
69. Bouët (1852, Part 3: 71).
70. Ibid.
71. Nardin (1967: 100).
72. Vallon (1861: 350).
73. Répin (1863: 92).
74. Burton (1864, Vol. I: 266).
75. Dalzel (1793/1853: x–xi). See also Alpern (1998).
76. Duncan (1847: 261).
77. Foa (1895: 259–260).
78. Forbes (1851, Vol. 2: 61).
79. Burton (1864, Vol. 2: 77).
80. Maroukis (1974: 113).
81. Cornevin (1962: 116).
82. Burton (1864, Vol. 1: 272).
83. Forbes (1851, Vol. 2: 120–121).
84. Ibid. (Vol. 1: 76).
85. Norris (1789: 18).
86. Argyle (1966: 84).
87. Burton (1864, Vol. 2: 80).
88. Hurston (1979: 65).

Chapter 2

1. M'Leod (1820: 37).
2. Akinjogbin (1967: 11); Yoder (1974).
3. Akinjogbin (1967: 105–109).

4. Ibid.: 62.

5. With his linguist's ear, Burton insisted that it should be pronounced "Hwedah," and phonetically, he was correct (Burton, 1864, Vol. 1: 61).

6. Akinjogbin (1967: 70–71).

7. Bay (1998: 59).

8. Quoted in Dalzel (1793/1853: 219).

9. Burton (1864, Vol. 1: 371).

10. Forbes (1851).

11. Norris (1789: 14).

12. Dalzel (1793/1853: 14–15).

13. Snelgrave (1734: 75).

14. Ibid.: 134.

15. Van Dantzig (1978: 295).

16. Akinjogbin (1967: 115–117).

17. Ibid.: 117.

18. Norris (1789: 127–128).

19. Akinjogbin (1967: 135).

20. Ibid.: 319.

21. Norris (1789: vii–ix).

22. Akinjogbin (1967: 137).

23. Polanyi (1966).

24. Freeman (1968: 270), a half-African missionary, was troubled by these practices but impressed by the virtual absence of crime in Dahomey.

25. Gautier (1935: 129–130).

26. Bay (1998) questioned the authority and even the existence of this official.

27. Valdez (1861: 342).

28. Bay (1998: 149).

29. Foa (1895: 265).

30. Burton (1864, Vol. 1: 263).

31. Yoder (1974).

32. Bay (1998: 177).

33. Bay (1977: 111).

34. Yoder (1974: 418).

35. Ibid.: 422.

36. Forbes (1851, Vol. 2: 139–140).

37. Yoder (1974).

38. Bay (1983).

39. Bay (1977: 22).

40. Polanyi (1966: 57); Alpern speculated that the Dahomean reverence for twins emerged because Wegbaja's son, Akaba, had a twin sister who may have ruled briefly after his death (1998: 22). This seems an unlikely origin for such a deeply held sentiment. See Mercier (1954).

41. Herskovits (1938, Vol. 2: 263).

42. Mercier (1954: 219).

43. Snelgrave (1734: 154).

44. Bay (1998: 158).

45. Pires (1957: 71).

46. M'Leod (1820: 39).

47. Bosman (1721: 363).

48. Akinjogbin (1967: 186–187).

49. Bay (1998: 179).

50. M'Leod (1820: 42–43).

51. Forbes (1851, Vol. 1: 33); Akinjogbin (1967: 197).

52. Labarthe (1803: 48).

53. M'Leod (1820: 48).

54. Duncan (1847, Vol. 1: 275).

55. Bay (1977: 21).

56. M'Leod (1820: 50); Labarthe (1803).

57. Herskovits (1938, Vol. 1: 85–86).

58. Bay (1998: 245).

59. Argyle (1966: 60).

60. Smith (1744/1967: 198).

61. Bay (1977: 297).

62. Bay (1983: 350).

63. Argyle (1966: 60).

64. Skertchly (1874: 455).

65. Hazoumé (1938: 130–131).

66. Bay (1983: 358).

67. Dalzel (1793/1853: 211).

68. Chaudoin (1891: 269–270).

69. Bay (1983: 359).

70. Argyle (1966: 55).

71. Bay (1977: 231).

72. Bay (1983: 360).

73. Ibid.: 262.

74. Bosman (1721: 318).

75. Herskovits (1938, Vol. 1: 30).

76. Dalzel (1793/1853: vii).

77. Herskovits (1938, Vol. 1: 39).

78. Bay (1998: 197).

79. Herskovits (1938, Vol. 1: 41–42).

80. Dalzel (1793/1853: xvii).

81. Forbes (1851, Vol. 1: 51).

82. Herskovits (1938, Vol. 1: 82).

83. Polanyi (1966: 84).

84. Dalzel (1793/1853: xxii).

85. Norris (1789: 64).

86. Ibid.: 64.

87. Ibid.: 65.

88. Herskovits (1938, Vol. 1: 90–91).

89. Forbes (1851: 175–176).

90. Ibid.: 36–37.

91. Herskovits (1938, Vol. 1: 115).

92. Mercier (1954).

93. Herskovits (1938, Vol. 1: 238).

94. Ibid.: 279–280.

95. Skertchly (1874: 439–440).

96. Herskovits (1938, Vol. 1: 343).

97. Mercier (1954: 219).

98. Ibid.: 214.

99. Smith (1744/1967: 197).

100. Herskovits (1938, Vol. 2: 125).

101. Ibid.: 229.

102. Mercier (1954: 228–229).

103. Maupoil (1988).

Chapter 3

1. Lombard (1967: 90).

2. Bay (1983: 341).

3. Norris (1789: vi). See also Bay (1998:30).

4. Le Hérrisé (1911: 26).

5. Norris (1789: 246).

6. Duncan (1847, Vol. 1: 221).

7. Valdez (1861: 332).

8. Skertchly (1874: 148).

9. Dalzel (1853: xv).

10. Duncan (1847, Vol. 1: 258).

11. Forbes (1851, Vol. 1: 82–83).

12. Smith (1744/1967: 186).

13. Ibid.: 182.

14. Ibid.: 183–184.

15. Ibid.: 192.

16. Snelgrave (1734: 80).

17. Ibid.: 80.

18. Norris (1789: ix).

19. Ibid.: 106.

20. Ibid.: 107.

21. Ibid.: 108.

22. Ibid.: 112.

23. Burton (1864, Vol. 1: 316).

24. Ibid.: 319–320.

25. Alpern (1998: 109).

26. Borghero (1997: no. 202, 225).

27. Burton (1864, Vol. 1: 228).

28. Skertchly (1874: 231).

29. Vallon (1861: 349).

30. Répin (1863: 92–93).

31. Forbes (1851, Vol. 2: 92).

32. Burton (1864, Vol. 1: 350).

33. Norris (1789, 100–101).

34. Burton (1864, Vol. 1: 355).

35. Ibid.: 362.

36. Ibid.: 363.

37. Bosman (1721: 231).

38. Snelgrave (1734: 43–44).

39. Ibid.: 44.

40. Ibid.: 47.

41. Ibid.: 52.

42. Duncan (1847: 252).

43. Burton (1864, Vol. 2: 59).

44. Bay (1977) questioned the existence of a "bush king," but it is evident that someone in addition to the king did conduct "customs."

45. Dalzel (1793/1853: 147).

46. Ibid.

47. Ibid.: 171.

48. Ibid.: 172.

49. Ibid.: 221.

50. Ibid.: 222.

51. Cruickshank (1848: 187).

52. Forbes (1851, Vol. 2: 32).

53. Law (1985: 83).

54. Maroukis (1974: 72).

55. Ibid.

56. Burton (1864, Vol. 2: 359).

57. Ibid.: 117.

58. Skertchly (1874: 46).

59. Dalzel (1793/1853: 205).

60. Herskovits (1938, Vol. 1: 228–229).

61. Maroukis (1974: 73).

62. Garcia (1988: 229); Morton-Williams (1993: 115).

Chapter 4

1. Forbes (1851, Vol. 2: 108).

2. Akinjogbin (1967).

3. Biobaku (1957: 42).

4. Forbes (1851, Vol. 2: 92–93).

5. Ibid.: 109.

6. Yoder (1974: 427).

7. Forbes (1851, Vol. 2 103).

8. Law (1993: 254).

166 *Notes*

9. Bowen (1857: 116).

10. Biobaku (1957: 44); Bowen (1857: 117).

11. Tucker (1858). Miss Tucker wrote from secondhand missionary sources. She did not visit Africa.

12. Biobaku (1957: 44); Johnson (1937).

13. Ajayi and Smith (1964: 39).

14. Laffin (1967: 48–49).

15. Tucker (1858).

16. Bowen (1857: 120).

17. Ajayi and Smith (1964: 50).

18. Townsend (1887: 80).

19. Johnson (1937: 77).

20. Ajayi and Smith (1964: 50).

21. Dunglas (1949: 39–40).

22. Burton (1864, Vol. 2: 269).

23. Ibid.: 270.

24. Ibid.: 309.

25. Dunglas (1949: 52).

26. Ibid.: 57.

27. Ibid.: 54.

28. Biobaku (1957: 74).

29. d'Almeida-Topor (1984: 145).

30. Garcia (1988: 133).

31. Ibid.: 129.

32. Obichere (1971: 63).

33. Ibid.: 295.

34. Chaudoin (1891).

35. Alpern (1998: 196); Schneider (1982: 136).

36. d'Almeida-Topor (1984: 142–143).

37. Schneider (1982: 46).

38. Ibid.: 165.

39. Martyn (1911: 233).

40. Garcia (1988: 134).

41. Maroukis (1974: 243–245).

42. Chaudoin (1891: 186–187).

43. Ibid.

44. Nuëlito (1897: 169).
45. Maroukis (1974: 247).
46. Nuëlito (1897: 170).
47. Burdo (1890: 90).
48. Le Hérrisé (1911: 114).
49. Nuëlito (1897: 165).
50. Ibid.: 184.
51. Johnson (1937: 455).
52. Maroukis (1974: 255).
53. Obichere (1971: 81).
54. Maroukis (1974: 114).
55. Maroukis (1974: 263–264); Garcia (1988: 95).
56. Maroukis (1974: 281).
57. Grandin (1895, Vol. 2: 61).
58. Martyn (1911: 193).
59. Morienval (1893: 150).
60. Martyn (1911); Mercer (1964).
61. Bern (1893: 261).
62. Porch (1991: 261).
63. Mercer (1964: 171).
64. d'Almeida-Topor (1984: 75).
65. Grandin (1895, Vol. 2: 107).
66. Martyn (1911: 206–207).
67. Turnbull (1964: 104).
68. Mercer (1964: 177).
69. Ibid.: 176–177.
70. Obichere (1971: 107).
71. Martyn (1911: 209).
72. Garcia (1988: 139).
73. Martyn (1911: 224).
74. Turnbull (1964: 106).
75. Martyn (1911: 224).
76. Turnbull (1964: 347).
77. Martyn (1911: 231).
78. Ibid.: 232.
79. Garcia (1988: 171).

80. Martyn (1911: 207–208).
81. Ibid.: 238.
82. Schelameur (1896: 118–119).
83. Alpern (1998: 155).
84. Morton-Williams (1993: 114).
85. d'Almeida-Topor (1984: 126).
86. Martyn (1911: 249).
87. Mercer (1964: 178).
88. Wellard (1974: 64).
89. Morton-Williams (1993: 113).
90. Newbury (1960: 152).
91. Le Hérrisé (1911: 68–69).
92. Degbelo (1989: 161).
93. Schneider (1982: 147).
94. Ibid.: 144.
95. Ibid.: 185.
96. d'Almeida-Topor (1984: 144–145).
97. Gorer (1935: 195–196).

Chapter 5

1. Manning (1990: 67–68).
2. Garcia (1984); Glélé (1974).
3. Simoons (1961: 10).
4. Edgerton (1971: 114).
5. Grinnell (1922: 156).
6. Roth (1899: 114); Plomley (1966: 135).
7. Shostak (1983).
8. Lindenbaum (1977).
9. Levine (1988).
10. Hayden (1862).
11. Grinnell (1923, Vol. 2: 127).
12. Ibid.: 128–129.
13. Ibid.: Vol. 1: 156.
14. Coquery-Vidrovitch (1997).
15. Sacks (1979).

16. See, for example, Sacks (1979), Sanday (1981), and Whyte (1978).

17. For a discussion of male dominance, see Whyte (1978), Harris (1993), and Ghiglieri (1999).

18. There is an enormous scholarly literature on this question. For a sampling, consult Barkow et al. (1992), Betzig (1997), Buss and Malamuth (1996), Eibl-Eibesfeldt (1989), Konner (1982), and Smuts (1996).

19. Wrangham and Peterson (1996); Ghiglieri (1999).

20. De Waal and Lanting (1997) and Smuts (1996) believe that male bonobos are less aggressive than *pan troglodytes*. Stanford (1998) expressed reservations about this view, as did Ghiglieri (1999).

21. For an introduction to this large and growing body of work, readers might consult Barkow et al. (1992), Blum (1997), Buss (1994), Gazzaniga (1992), and Konner (1982).

22. Burton (1995: 115).

23. Nadeau (1996).

24. Davis (1975).

25. Harris (1993); Sacks (1979); Sanday (1981).

26. Sanday (1981: 210–211).

27. Edgerton and Conant (1964).

28. Ardener (1973).

29. Coquery-Vidrovich (1997).

30. Cook (1991: 151).

31. Ibid.: 153.

32. Ibid.: 154.

33. Smith (1965: 68).

34. Amadiume (1987: 67).

35. Ibid.: 33.

36. Lebeuf (1963).

37. Binns (1975: 118).

38. Edgerton (1995).

39. Pospisil (1963: 59).

40. Meggitt (1977: 99).

41. Bamberger (1974).

42. Brown (1975). A recent survey reported that Iroquois women never went to war (Adams 1983). That is not correct.

43. Keeley (1996: 87).

44. Lowie (1935: 215).

45. Medicine (1983).

46. Landes (1968: 39).

47. Ibid.: 144.

48. Lewis (1941).

49. Kleinbaum (1983: 131).

50. Dobrizhoffer (1822, Vol. 2: 423).

51. Jones (1997: 77).

52. Ibid.: 49.

53. Jancar (1988: 47).

54. Griesse and Stites (1982: 73).

55. Cottam (1983a).

56. Saywell (1985).

57. Ibid.: 168.

58. Jorgensen (1994: 289).

59. Tétreault (1994).

60. Edgerton (1989: 128).

61. Duiker (1982: 119).

62. Dahn (1966).

63. Salaff and Merkle (1973).

64. Li (1993, 1994).

65. Dajia (1994).

66. Kozaryn (1998).

67. For an account of the death of a woman naval aviator, see Spears (1998).

68. Tyson (1998).

69. Ilesanmi (1992: 90).

70. Wekesser and Polesetsky (1991).

71. Addis et al. (1994).

72. Mitchell (1989); Moskos and Wood (1988).

73. Miller (1995).

74. Maccoby and Jacklin (1974: 242–243).

75. Bjorkvist and Niemelä (1992); Blum (1997).

76. Nisbett and Cohen (1996: 87–88).

77. *The Sunday Times* (London), 3 December 1995.

78. Cottam (1983a: 146).

79. Wekesser and Polesetsky (1991: 32).
80. Mitchell (1989).
81. Herbert (1988).
82. Disher (1998: 291).
83. Saywell (1985).
84. Addis et al. (1994); Weinstein and White (1997).
85. Enloe (1999); Miller (1995).

Bibliography

Adams, D. B. "Why There Are So Few Women Warriors." *Behavior Science Research,* 18:196–212, 1983.

Addis, E., V. E. Russo, and L. Sebesta (eds.). *Women Soldiers: Images and Realities.* New York: St. Martin's Press, 1994.

Ajayi, J. F. A., and I. Espie (eds.). *A Thousand Years of West African History.* London: Nelson, 1965.

Ajayi, J. F. A., and R. Smith. *Yoruba Warfare in the Nineteenth Century.* Cambridge: Cambridge University Press, 1964.

Akinjogbin, I. A. "Archibald Dalzel: Slave Trader and Historian of Dahomey." *Journal of African History,* 7:67–78, 1966.

_____. *Dahomey and Its Neighbors: 1708–1818.* Cambridge: Cambridge University Press, 1967.

Alpern, S. B. *Amazons of Black Sparta: The Women Warriors of Dahomey.* New York: New York University Press, 1998.

Amadiume, I. *Male Daughters, Female Husbands: Gender and Sex in an African Society.* London: Zed Books, 1987.

Ardener, S. "Sexual Insult and Female Militancy." *Man,* 8:422–440, 1973.

Argyle, W. J. *The Fon of Dahomey: A History and Ethnography of the Old Kingdom.* Oxford: Clarendon Press, 1966.

Aublet, E. *La Guerre au Dahomey, 1888–1893.* Paris: Berger-Levrault, 1894.

Bamberger, J. "The Myth of Matriarchy: Why Men Rule in Primitive Society." In M. Z. Rosaldo and L. Lamphere (eds.), *Women, Culture, and Society.* Stanford: Stanford University Press, 1974. Pp. 263–280.

Barbou, A. *Histoire de la guerre au Dahomey.* Paris: Librairie Dusquesne, 1893.

Barkow, J. H. *Darwin, Sex and Status: Biological Approaches to Mind and Culture.* Toronto: University of Toronto Press, 1989.

Barkow, J. H., L. Cosmides, and J. Tooby (eds.). *The Adapted Mind: Evolutionary Psychology and the Generation of Culture.* New York: Oxford University Press, 1992.

Bay, E. G. *The Royal Women of Abomey.* Ph.D. dissertation, Boston University, 1977.

———. "Servitude and Worldly Success in the Palace of Dahomey." In C. C. Robinson and M. A. Klein (eds.), *Women and Slavery in Africa.* Madison: University of Wisconsin Press, 1983. Pp. 340–367.

———. *Wives of the Leopard: Gender, Politics and Culture in the Kingdom of Dahomey.* Charlottesville: University of Virginia Press, 1998.

Bayol, M. J. "Les Forces militaires actuelles du Dahomey." *Revue Scientifique,* 49:520–524, 1892.

Bern, J. *L'Expédition du Dahomey (août-décembre 1892): Notes éparses d'un voluntaire.* Sidi-Bel-Abbès, Algeria: Ch. Lavenne, 1893.

Betzig, L. (ed.). *Human Nature: A Critical Reader.* New York: Oxford University Press, 1997.

Binns, C. T. *The Warrior People: Zulu Origins, Customs and Witchcraft.* London: Robert Hale, 1975.

Biobaku, S. O. *The Egba and Their Neighbours, 1842–1872.* Oxford: Clarendon, 1957.

Bjorkqvist, K., and P. Niemelä (eds.). *Of Mice and Women: Aspects of Female Aggression.* New York: Academic Press, 1992.

Blond, G. *Histoire de la Légion Étrangere, 1831–1981.* Paris: Plon, 1964.

Blum, Deborah. *Sex on the Brain: The Biological Difference Between Men and Women.* New York: Viking, 1997.

Borghero, F. *Journal de Francesco Borghero, Premier Missionaire du Dahomey (1861–1865).* Renzo Mandirola and Yves Morel, eds. Paris: Karthala, 1997.

Bosman, W. *A New and Accurate Description of the Coast of Guinea, Divided into the Gold, the Slave, and the Ivory Coasts.* 2nd ed. London: J. Knapton, 1721.

Bouche, P. *La Côte de Esclaves et le Dahomey.* Paris: Librairie Plon, 1885.

Bouët, A. "Le Royaume de Dahomey," *L'Illustration,* 10(Part 3):71–74. 1852.

Bowen, T. J. *Adventures and Missionary Labors in Several Countries in the Interior of Africa from 1849 to 1856.* Charleston, SC: Southern Baptist Publication Society, 1857.

Brown, J. K. "Iroquois Women: An Ethnohistorical Note." In R. R. Reiter (ed.), *Toward an Anthropology of Women*. New York: Monthly Review Press, 1975. Pp. 235–251.

Burdo, A. "Au Dahomey." *Journal des Voyages*, no. 683 (August 10, 1890).

Burton, N. "Trends in Mathematics Achievement for Young Men and Women." In I. M. Carl (ed.), *Prospects for School Mathematics*. Reston, VA: National Council of Teachers of Mathematics, 1995. Pp. 115–127.

Burton, Sir R. *A Mission to Gelele, King of Dahome*, 2 vols. London: Tinsley Brothers, 1864.

Buss, D. M. *The Evolution of Desire: Strategies of Human Mating*. New York: Basic Books, 1994.

Buss, D. M., and N. M. Malamuth (eds.). *Sex, Power, Conflict: Evolution and Feminist Perspectives*. New York: Oxford University Press, 1996.

Cairns, H. A. C. *Prelude to Imperialism*. London: Routledge, 1965.

Campbell, P. B. "Redefining the 'Girl Problem' in Mathematics." In W. G. Secada, E. Feunema, L. B. Adajian (eds.), *New Directions for Equity in Mathematics Education*. Cambridge: Cambridge University Press, 1995. Pp. 225–241.

Carlyle, T. "Occasional Discourse on the Nigger Question." *Fraser's Magazine*, 40:670–679, 1849.

Chadwick, N. *The Celts*. London: Penguin, 1971.

Chaudoin, E. *Trois Mois de captivité au Dahomey*. Paris: Librairie Hachette, 1891.

Conneau, T. *A Slaver's Log Book of 20 Years' Residence in Africa*. Englewood Cliffs, NJ: Prentice-Hall, 1976.

Cook, H. B. K. *Small Town, Big Hell: An Ethnographic Study of Aggression in a Margarifeno Community*. Ph.D. dissertation, UCLA, 1991.

Coquery-Vidrovitch, C. *African Women: A Modern History*. Boulder, CO: Westview Press, 1997.

Cornevin, R. *Histoire du Dahomey*. Paris: Berger-Levrault, 1962.

Cornum, R. (as told to Peter Copeland). *She Went to War: The Rhonda Cornum Story*. Novato, CA: Presidio Press, 1992.

Cottam, K. J. (ed.). *The Golden-Tressed Soldier*. Manhattan, KS: MA/AH, 1983a.

Cottam, K. J. *Soviet Airwomen in Combat in World War II*. Manhattan, KS: MA/AH, 1983b.

Cruickshank, B. Report of 9 November 1848, PP, 1849 (Lords), xxviii (32), Appendix, p. 187.

_____. *Eighteen Years on the Gold Coast of Africa, Including an Account of the Native Tribes, and Their Intercourse with Europeans*, 2 vols. London: Hurst and Blackett, 1853.

Dahn, L. H. "The Long-Haired Army." *Vietnamese Studies*, 10:61–67, 1966.

Dajia, S. "Introduction of China's Female Generals." *Beijing Review*, 37:11–19, 1994.

d'Albéca, A. L. *La France au Dahomey*. Paris: Librairie Hachette, 1895.

d'Almeida-Topor, H. *Les Amazones*. Paris: Rochevignes, 1984.

Daly, M., and M. Wilson. *Homicide*. New York: Aldine de Gruyter, 1988.

Dalzel, A. *The History of Dahomy: An Inland Kingdom of Africa*. London: T. Spilsbury and Son, 1967 (orig. 1793).

Davidson, B. *The African Genius: An Introduction to African Social and Cultural History*. Boston: Little, Brown, 1969.

Davidson, B., and F. K. Buah. *The Growth of African Civilisation: A History of West Africa 1000–1800*. London: Longmans, 1965.

Davis, N. Z. *Society and Culture in Early Modern France*. Stanford: Stanford University Press, 1975.

Davis-Kimball, J. "Warrior Women of the Eurasian Steppes." *Archeology*, 50:44–48, 1997.

Degbelo, A. "Les Amazones du Danxomé, 1645–1900." *Mémoire de maîtrise d'histoire*, Université Nationale de Benin, 1989.

De Pauw, L. G. *Battle Cries and Lullabies: Women in War from Prehistory to the Present*. Norman: University of Oklahoma Press, 1998.

De Salinis, A. *Campagne de "La Naïade" (1890–1892): La Marine au Dahomey*. Paris: Librairie L. Sanard, 1901.

De Waal, F., and F. Lanting. *Bonobo: The Forgotten Ape*. Berkeley: University of California Press, 1997.

Disher, S. H. *First Class: Women Join the Ranks at the Naval Academy*. Annapolis, MD: Naval Institute Press, 1998.

Dobrizhoffer, M. *An Account of the Abipones, an Equestrian People of Paraguay*, 3 vols. London: John Murray, 1822.

Duiker, W. J. "Vietnam: War of Insurgency." In N. L. Goldman (ed.), *Female Soldiers—Combatants or Noncombatants? Historical and Contemporary Perspectives*. Westport, CT: Greenwood Press, 1982. Pp. 107–122.

Duncan, J. *Travels in Western Africa in 1845 and 1846*, 2 vols. London: Richard Bentley, 1847.

Dunglas, E. "Deuxième Attaque de Dahoméens contre Abeokuta (15 mars 1864)." *Études Dahoméens*, 2:37–58, 1949.

Edgerton, R. B. *The Individual in Cultural Adaptation*. Berkeley: University of California Press, 1971.

———. *Mau Mau: An African Crucible*. New York: The Free Press, 1989.

———. *The Fall of the Asante Empire*. New York: The Free Press, 1995.

Edgerton, R. B., and F. P. Conant. "Kilapat: The 'Shaming Party' Among the Pokot of East Africa." *Southwestern Journal of Anthropology*, 20:404–418, 1964.

Eibl-Eibesfeldt, I. *Human Ethology*. New York: Aldine de Gruyter, 1989.

Ellis, W. *Polynesian Researches: Hawaii*. (New edition, enlarged and improved). Rutland, VT: Charles E. Tuttle, 1969.

Elshtain, J. B. *Women and War*. New York: Basic Books, 1987.

Enloe, C. *Maneuvers: The International Politics of Militarizing Women's Lives*. Berkeley: University of California Press, 1999.

Fage, J. D. "Slavery and the Slave Trade in the Context of West African History." *Journal of African History*, 10:393–404, 1969.

———. *A History of West Africa: An Introductory Survey*, 4th ed. Aldershot: Gregg Revivals, 1992.

Foa, E. *Le Dahomey*. Paris: A. Henneyer, 1895.

Forbes, F. E. *Dahomey and the Dahomans*, 2 vols. London: Longman, Brown, Green, and Longmans, 1851.

Freeman, T. B. *Journal of Various Visits to the Kingdoms of Ashanti, Aku, and Dahomi in Western Africa*, 3rd ed. London: Cass, 1968 (orig. 1844).

Garcia, L. *Le Royaume du Dahomé: Face à la pénétracion coloniale: Affrontements et incompréhension (1875–1894)*. Paris: Karthala, 1988.

Gautier, E. F. *L'Afrique Noire Occidentale*. Paris: Librairie Larose, 1935.

Gazzaniga, M. *Nature's Mind: The Biological Roots of Thinking, Emotions, Sexuality, Language and Intelligence*. New York: Basic Books, 1992.

Ghiglieri, M. P. *The Dark Side of Man: Tracing the Origins of Male Violence*. Reading, MA: Persens Books, 1999.

Glélé, M. A. *La Danxome: Du Pouvoir Aja à la nation Fon*. Paris: Nubia, 1974.

Gorer, G. *Africa Dances: A Book About West African Negroes*. London: Faber & Faber, 1935.

Grandin, (Commandant). *Le Dahomey: À L'Assaut du pays des noirs*, 2 vols. Paris: Rene Haton Librairie-Editeur, 1895.

Griesse, A. E., and R. Stites. "Russia: Revolution and War." In N. L. Goldman (ed.), *Female Soldiers—Combatants or Noncombatants? Historical and Contemporary Perspectives*. Newport, CT: Greenwood Press, 1982. Pp. 61–84.

Grinnell, G. B. *The Cheyenne Indians: Their History and Ways of Life*, 2 vols. Lincoln: University of Nebraska Press, 1923.

Guillevin, M. *Voyage dans l'intérieur du royaume de Dahomey*. Paris: Librairie de la Société de Géographic, 1862.

Harris, M. *Culture, Man, and Nature: An Introduction to General Anthropology*. New York: Thomas Y. Crowell, 1971.

_____. *Culture, People, Nature: An Introduction to General Anthropology*. New York: HarperCollins, 1993.

Hayden, F. V. *Contributions to the Ethnography and Philology of the Indian Tribes of the Missouri Valley*, Vol. 12. Philadelphia: American Philosophical Society Transactions, N. S., 1862.

Hazoumé, P. "Tata Ajachê soupo ma ha awouinyan." *La Reconaissance Africaine*, Parts 1–3: 1: 7–9, 2: 7–8, 3: 7–8, 1925.

_____. *Doguicimi*. Paris: Larose, 1938.

Herbert, M. S. *Camouflage Isn't Only for Combat: Gender, Sexuality and Women in the Military*. New York: New York University Press, 1988.

Herskovits, M. J. *Dahomey: An Ancient West African Kingdom*, 2 vols. New York: Augustin, 1938.

Hurston, Z. N. *I Love Myself, When I am Laughing . . .* Old Westbury, NY: Feminist Press, 1979.

Ilesanmi, T. M. "The Yoruba Worldview on Women and Warfare." In T. Falola and R. Law (eds.), *Warfare and Diplomacy in Precolonial Nigeria*. Madison: University of Wisconsin Press, 1992. Pp. 199–207.

Isichei, E. *History of West Africa Since 1800*. New York: Africana, 1977.

Jancar, B. "Women Soldiers in Yugoslavia's National Liberation Struggle, 1941–1945." In E. Isaksson (ed.), *Women and the Military System*. New York: Harvester: Wheatsheaf, 1988. Pp. 47–67.

Johnson, M. "News from Nowhere: Duncan and 'Adofuodia.'" *History in Africa*, 1:55–66, 1974.

Johnson, S. *The History of the Yorubas from the Earliest Times to the Beginning of the British Protectorate.* London: Church Missionary Society, 1937.

Jones, D. E. *Women Warriors: A History.* Washington, DC: Brassey's, 1997.

Jorgensen, C. "Women, Revolution, and Israel." In M. A. Tétreault (ed.), *Women and Revolution in Africa, Asia, and the New World.* Columbia: University of South Carolina Press, 1994. Pp. 272–296.

Kea, R. A. "Firearms and Warfare on the Gold and Slave Coasts from the Sixteenth to the Nineteenth Centuries." *Journal of African History,* 12:185–213, 1971.

Keegan, J. *A History of Warfare.* New York: Knopf, 1993.

Keeley, L. H. *War Before Civilization: The Myth of the Peaceful Savage.* New York: Oxford University Press, 1996.

Keil, S. V. W. *Those Wonderful Women in Their Flying Machines.* New York: Rawson, Wade, 1979.

Kirsta, A. *Deadlier than the Male: Violence and Aggression Among Women.* New York: HarperCollins, 1994.

Kleinbaum, A. W. *The War Against the Amazons.* New York: McGraw-Hill, 1983.

Konner, M. J. *The Tangled Web: Biological Constraints on the Human Spirit.* New York: Harper Colophon Books, 1982.

Kozaryn, L. D. "Making a Place for NATO's Military Women." *American Forces Information Service News Articles,* April 1998.

Labarthe, P. *Voyage à la Côte de Guinée.* Paris: Debray Librairie, 1803.

Laffin, J. *Women in Battle.* London: Abelard-Schuman, 1967.

Laffitte, M. *Le Dahomé: Souvenirs de voyage et de mission.* Tours: Alfred Mame, 1873.

Landes, R. *The Mystic Lake Sioux: Sociology of the Mdewakantonwan Santee.* Madison: University of Wisconsin Press, 1968.

Law, R. "Human Sacrifice in Pre-colonial West Africa." *African Affairs,* 84:53–88, 1985.

Law, R. "'My Head Belongs to the King': On the Political and Ritual Significance of Decapitation in Pre-Colonial Dahomey." *Journal of African History,* 30:399–415, 1989.

_____. "The Oyo-Dahomey Wars, 1726–1823: A Military Analysis." In T. Falola and R. Law (eds.), *Warfare and Diplomacy in Precolonial Nigeria.* Madison: University of Wisconsin Press, 1992. Pp. 9–25.

_____. "The 'Amazons' of Dahomey." *Paideuma,* 39:245–260, 1993.

Lebeuf, A. M. D. "The Role of Women in the Political Organization of African Societies." In D. Paulme (ed.), *Women of Tropical Africa.* Berkeley: University of California Press, 1963. Pp. 93–119.

Le Hérrisé, A. *L'ancien royaume du Dahomey.* Paris: E. Larose, 1911.

Leith-Ross, S. *African Women: A Study of the Ibo of Nigeria.* London: Faber and Faber, 1939.

Levine, N. E. *The Dynamics of Polyandry: Kinship, Domesticity, and Population on the Tibetan Border.* Berkeley: University of California Press, 1988.

LeVine, V. T. "The Coups in Upper Volta, Dahomey, and the Central African Republic." In R. I. Rotberg and A. A. Mazrui (eds.), *Protest and Power in Black Africa.* New York: Oxford University Press, 1970. Pp. 1035–1071.

Levtzion, N. "The Thirteenth- and Fourteenth-Century Kings of Mali." *Journal of African History,* 4:341–353, 1963.

Lewis, O. "Manly-Hearted Women Among the North Piegan." *American Anthropologist,* 43:173–187, 1941.

Li, X. "Chinese Women in the People's Liberation Army: Professionals or Quasi-Professionals?" *Armed Forces and Society,* 20:69–83, 1993.

_____. "Chinese Women Soldiers: A History of 5,000 Years." *Social Education,* 58:67–71, 1994.

Lindendaum, S. *Kuru Sorcery: Disease and Danger in the New Guinea Highlands.* Palo Alto, CA: Mayfield, 1977.

Lloyd, P. C. "Sacred Kingship and Government Among the Yoruba." *Africa,* 30:121–237, 1960.

Lombard, J. "The Kingdom of Dahomey." In D. Forde and P. M. Kaberry (eds.), *West African Kingdoms in the Nineteenth Century.* London: Oxford University Press, 1967. Pp. 70–92.

Lowie, R. H. *The Crow Indians.* New York: Rinehart, 1935.

Maccoby, E., and C. Jacklin. *The Psychology of Sex Differences.* Stanford, CA: Stanford University Press, 1974.

Macdonald, S., P. Holden, and S. Ardener (eds.). *Images of Women in Peace and War: Cross-Cultural and Historical Perspectives*. London: Macmillan, 1987.

Manning, P. *Slavery, Colonialism and Economic Growth in Dahomey, 1640–1960*. Cambridge: Cambridge University Press, 1982.

_____. *Slavery and African Life*. Cambridge: Cambridge University Press, 1990.

Marceau, (Captain). *Le Tirailleur Soudanais*. Paris: Berger-Levrault, 1911.

Markale, J. *Women of the Celts*. Rochester, VT: Inner Traditions International, 1986.

Maroukis, T. C. *Warfare and Society in the Kingdom of Dahomey: 1818–1894*. Ph.D. dissertation, Boston University, 1974.

Martyn, F. *Life in the Legion from a Soldier's Point of View*. New York: Scribner's, 1911.

Maupoil, B. *La Géomancie à l'ancienne Côte des Esclaves*. Paris: Institut d'Ethnologie, 1988.

McIntosh, E. P. *Sisterhood of Spies: The Women of the OSS*. Annapolis, MD: Naval Institute Press, 1998.

McLeave, H. *The Damned Die Hard*. New York: Saturday Review Press, 1973.

Medicine, B. "'Warrior Women'—Sex Role Alternatives for Plains Indian Women." In P. Albers and B. Medicine (eds.), *The Hidden Half: Studies of Plains Indian Women*. Washington, DC: University Press of America, 1983. Pp. 267–280.

Meggitt, M. *Blood Is Their Argument: Warfare Among the Mae Enga Tribesmen of the New Guinea Highlands*. Palo Alto, CA: Mayfield, 1977.

Mercer, C. *The Foreign Legion: The Vivid History of a Unique Military Tradition*. London: Arthur Barker, 1964.

Mercier, P. "The Fon of Dahomey." In D. Forde (ed.), *African Worlds: Studies in the Cosmological Ideas and Social Values of African Peoples*. London: Oxford University Press, 1954. Pp. 210–234.

Miller, J. C. "Nzinga of Matamba in a New Perspective." *Journal of African History*, 16:201–216, 1975.

Miller, L. *Feminism and the Exclusion of Army Women from Combat*. Cambridge, MA: John M. Olin Institute for Strategic Studies, 1995.

Mitchell, B. *Weak Link: The Feminization of the American Military.* Washington, DC: Regnery Gateway, 1989.

M'Leod, J. *A Voyage to Africa: with Some Account of the Manners and Customs of the Dahomian People.* London: John Murray, 1820.

Montagu, A. *The Natural Superiority of Women.* New York: Macmillan, 1953.

Moore, E. O. *History of Abeokuta.* London: Richard Clay and Sons, 1916.

Morienval, H. *La Guerre du Dahomey. Journal de campagne d'un sous-lieutenant d'infanterie de marine.* Paris: Berger-Levrault, 1893.

Morton-Williams, P. "A Yoruba Woman Remembers Servitude in a Palace of Dahomey, in the Reigns of Kings Glele and Behanzin." *Africa,* 63:102–117, 1993.

Moskos, C. C., and F. R. Wood (eds.). *The Military: More than Just a Job?* Washington, DC: Pergamon-Brassey's, 1988.

Myles, B. *Night Witches: The Untold Story of Soviet Women in Combat.* Novato, CA: Presidio Press, 1981.

Nabors, R. L. "Women in the Army: Do They Measure Up?" *Military Review,* 62:50–61, October 1982.

Nadeau, R. L. *S/He Brain: Science, Sexual Politics, and the Myths of Feminism.* Westport, CT: Praeger, 1996.

Nardin, J-C. "La Reprise des relations franco-dahoméennes au XIXe siècle. La Mission d'Auguste Bouët à la cour d'Abomey." *Cahiers d'études africaines,* 7:59–126, 1967.

Newbury, C. C. "An Early Inquiry into Slavery and Captivity in Dahomey." *Zaire,* 15:53–67, 1960.

Niethammer, C. *Daughters of the Earth.* New York: Macmillan, 1977.

Nisbett, R. E., and D. Cohen. *Culture of Honor: The Psychology of Violence in the South.* Boulder, CO: Westview Press, 1996.

Noir, L. *Au Dahomey: Une Amazone de Behanzin.* Paris: A. Fayard, n.d.

Norris, R. *Memoirs of the Reign of Bossa Ahadee, King of Dahomey.* London: W. Lowndes, 1789.

Nuëlito, E. *Au Dahomey: Journal d'un officier de Spahis.* Abbeville: C. Paillart, 1897.

Obichere, B. I. *West African States and European Expansion: the Dahomey-Niger Hinterland, 1885–1898.* New Haven: Yale University Press, 1971.

Oliver, R. *The African Experience.* London: Weidenfeld and Nicolson, 1991.

Otterbein, K. F. *The Evolution of War*. New Haven: Human Relations Area Files, 1985.

_____. "The Origins of War." *Critical Review*, 11:251–278, 1997.

Oyewùmí, O. *The Invention of Women: Making an African Sense of Western Gender Discourses*. Minneapolis: University of Minnesota Press, 1997.

Palau-Marty, M. *Le Roi-Dieu du Benin*. Paris: Berger-Levrault, 1964.

Penzer, N. M. (ed.). *Selected Papers on Anthropology, Travel and Exploration by Sir Richard Burton, K.C.M.G*. New York: Robert M. McBride, 1924.

Pires, V. F. *Crônica de uma Embaixada Luso-Brasileira à Costa d'África em fins do século XVIII, incluindo texto da Viegem de África em o reino de Dahomé*. São Paulo: Companhia Editora Nacional, 1957.

Plomley, N. J. B. *Friendly Mission: The Tasmanian Journal and Papers of George Augustus Robinson, 1829–1834*. Hobart: Tasmania Historical Research Association, 1966.

Poirier, Jules. *Campagne du Dahomey, 1892–1894*. Paris: H. Charles-Lavauzelle, 1895.

Polanyi, K. *Dahomey and the Slave Trade: Analysis of an Archaic Economy*. Seattle: University of Washington Press, 1966.

Porch, D. *The French Foreign Legion: A Complete History of the Legendary Fighting Force*. New York: HarperCollins, 1991.

Pospisil, L. *The Kapauku Papuans of West New Guinea*. New York: Holt, Rinehart and Winston, 1963.

Prévaudeau, M-M. *Abomey—La-Mystique*. Bruxelles: La Renaissance du Livre, 1936.

Quénum, M. *Les Ancêtres de la famille Quénum*. Laugres: Dominique Guéniot, 1981.

Reader, J. *Africa: A Biography of the Continent*. New York: Knopf, 1998.

Répin, A. "Voyage au Dahomey." *Le Tour du Monde*, 7:65–112, 1863.

Rice, E. *Captain Sir Richard Francis Burton*. New York: Scribner's, 1990.

Ridgway, A. R. "Journal of a Visit to Dahomey; or, the Snake Country, in the Months of March and April, 1847." *New Monthly Magazine and Humorist*, Vol. 81, Nos. 322–324:187–198, 299–309, 406–414, 1847.

Rogan, H. *Mixed Company: Women in the Modern Army*. Boston: Beacon Press, 1981.

Rolbant, S. *The Israeli Soldier: Profile of an Army*. New York: Thomas Yoseloff, 1970.

Ross, D. *The Autonomous Kingdom of Dahomey, 1818–1894*. Ph.D. dissertation, University of London, 1967.

_____. "Dahomey." In M. Crowder (ed.), *West African Resistance: The Military Response to Colonial Occupation*. London: Hutchinson, 1971. Pp. 144–169.

Roth, H. L. *The Aborigines of Tasmania*, 2nd ed. Halifax, Nova Scotia: F. King, 1899.

Sacks, K. *Sisters and Wives: The Past and Future of Sexual Equality*. Westport, CT: Greenwood Press, 1979.

Salaff, J., and J. Merkle. "Women and Revolution: The Lessons of the Soviet Union and China." In M. B. Young (ed.), *Women in China: Studies in Social Change and Feminism*. Ann Arbor: University of Michigan, Center for Chinese Studies, 1973. Pp. 145–177.

Sanday, P. R. *Female Power and Male Dominance: On the Origins of Sexual Inequality*. Cambridge: Cambridge University Press, 1981.

Sansom, G. B. *Japan: A Short Cultural History*. New York: Appleton-Century-Crofts, 1962.

Saywell, S. *Women in War*. New York: Viking, 1985.

Schelameur, F. *Souvenirs de la campagne du Dahomey*. Paris: H. Charles-Lavauzell, 1896.

Schneider, W. H. *An Empire for the Masses: The French Popular Image of Africa, 1870–1900*. Westport, CT: Greenwood Press, 1982.

Shostak, M. *Nisa: The Life and Words of a !Kung Woman*. Cambridge, MA: Harvard University Press, 1983.

Simoons, F. S. *Eat Not This Flesh: Food Avoidances in the Old World*. Madison: University of Wisconsin Press, 1961.

Skertchly, J. A. *Dahomey as It Is*. London: Chapman and Hall, 1874.

Smith, R. "The Alafin in Exile: A Study of the Igboho Period in Oyo History." *Journal of African History*, 6:57–77, 1965.

Smith, W. *A New Voyage to Guinea*. London: F. Cass, 1967 (orig. 1744).

Smuts, B. "Male Aggression Against Women: An Evolutionary Perspective." In D. M. Buss and N. M. Malamuth (eds.), *Sex, Power, Conflict: Evolutionary and Feminist Perspectives*. New York: Oxford, 1996. Pp. 231–268.

Snelgrave, W. *A New Account of Some Parts of Guinea, and the Slave Trade*. London: J. J. and P. Knapton, 1734.

Spears, S. *Call Sign Revlon: The Life and Death of Navy Fighter Pilot Kara Hultgreen*. Annapolis, MD: Naval Institute Press, 1998.

Stanford, C. B. "The Social Behavior of Chimpanzees and Bonobos: Empirical Evidence and Shifting Assumptions." *Current Anthropology,* 39:391–420, 1998.

Tétreault, M. A. (ed.). *Women and Revolution in Africa, Asia, and the New World.* Columbia: University of South Carolina Press, 1994.

Toutée, (Commandant). *Du Dahomey au Sahara: La Nature et l'homme.* Paris: Armand Colin, 1899.

Townsend, G. *Memoir of the Reverend Henry Townsend.* London: Marshall Brothers, 1887.

Tucker, M. *Abbeokuta.* London: James Nisbet, 1858.

Turnbull, P. *The Foreign Legion: A History of the Foreign Legion.* London: Heinemann, 1964.

Tyson, A. S. "A Few More Good Women." *Christian Science Monitor,* May 20, 1998, pp. 9–12.

Valdez, F. T. *Six Years of a Traveller's Life in Western Africa,* 2 vols. London: Hurst and Blackett, 1861.

Vallon, A. "Le Royaume de Dahomey." *Revue Maritime et Coloniale,* 3:329–358, 1861.

Van Creveld, M. "Why Israel Doesn't Send Women into Combat." *Parameters,* 23:5–9, 1993.

Van Dantzig, A. (ed.). *The Dutch and the Guinea Coast, 1674–1742: A Collection of Documents from the General State Archive at the Hague.* Acra, Ghana: Academy of Arts and Sciences, 1978.

Verdal, G. "Les Amazones du Dahomey." *L'Education Physique,* New Series, 32:52–59, 1934.

Weinstein, L., and C. C. White (eds.). *Wives and Warriors: Women and the Military in the United States and Canada.* Westport, CT: Bergin and Garvey, 1997.

Wekesser, C., and M. Polesetsky (eds.). *Women in the Military.* San Diego: Greenhaven Press, 1991.

Wellard, J. *The French Foreign Legion.* London: Deutsch, 1974.

Whyte, M. K. *The Status of Women in Pre-Industrial Society.* Princeton: University of Princeton Press, 1978.

Wrangham, R., and D. Peterson. *Demonic Males: Apes and the Origins of Human Nature.* Boston: Houghton Mifflin, 1996.

Yoder, J. C. "Fly and Elephant Parties: Political Polarization in Dahomey, 1840–1870." *Journal of African History,* 15:417–432, 1974.

Index

Index